"This series is a tremendous resource for those wanting to study and teach the Bible with an understanding of how the gospel is woven throughout Scripture. Here are gospel-minded pastors and scholars doing gospel business from all the Scriptures. This is a biblical and theological feast preparing God's people to apply the entire Bible to all of life with heart and mind wholly committed to Christ's priorities."

BRYAN CHAPELL, President Emeritus, Covenant Theological Seminary; Senior Pastor, Grace Presbyterian Church, Peoria, Illinois

"Mark Twain may have smiled when he wrote to a friend, 'I didn't have time to write you a short letter, so I wrote you a long letter.' But the truth of Twain's remark remains serious and universal, because well-reasoned, compact writing requires extra time and extra hard work. And this is what we have in the Crossway Bible study series *Knowing the Bible*. The skilled authors and notable editors provide the contours of each book of the Bible as well as the grand theological themes that bind them together as one Book. Here, in a 12-week format, are carefully wrought studies that will ignite the mind and the heart."

R. KENT HUGHES, Visiting Professor of Practical Theology, Westminster Theological Seminary

"*Knowing the Bible* brings together a gifted team of Bible teachers to produce a high-quality series of study guides. The coordinated focus of these materials is unique: biblical content, provocative questions, systematic theology, practical application, and the gospel story of God's grace presented all the way through Scripture."

PHILIP G. RYKEN, President, Wheaton College

"These *Knowing the Bible* volumes provide a significant and very welcome variation on the general run of inductive Bible studies. This series provides substantial instruction, as well as teaching through the very questions that are asked. *Knowing the Bible* then goes even further by showing how any given text links with the gospel, the whole Bible, and the formation of theology. I heartily endorse this orientation of individual books to the whole Bible and the gospel, and I applaud the demonstration that sound theology was not something invented later by Christians, but is right there in the pages of Scripture."

GRAEME L. GOLDSWORTHY, former lecturer, Moore Theological College; author, *According to Plan, Gospel and Kingdom, The Gospel in Revelation,* and *Gospel and Wisdom*

"What a gift to earnest, Bible-loving, Bible-searching believers! The organization and structure of the Bible study format presented through the *Knowing the Bible* series is so well conceived. Students of the Word are led to understand the content of passages through perceptive, guided questions, and they are given rich insights and application all along the way in the brief but illuminating sections that conclude each study. What potential growth in depth and breadth of understanding these studies offer! One can only pray that vast numbers of believers will discover more of God and the beauty of his Word through these rich studies."

BRUCE A. WARE, Professor of Christian Theology, The Southern Baptist Theological Seminary

KNOWING THE BIBLE

J. I. Packer, Theological Editor
Dane C. Ortlund, Series Editor
Lane T. Dennis, Executive Editor

•   •   •   •   •   •

Genesis	Psalms	Jonah, Micah, and Nahum	Ephesians
Exodus	Proverbs		Philippians
Leviticus	Ecclesiastes	Haggai, Zechariah, and Malachi	Colossians and Philemon
Numbers	Song of Solomon		
Deuteronomy	Isaiah	Matthew	1–2 Thessalonians
Joshua	Jeremiah	Mark	1–2 Timothy and Titus
Judges	Lamentations, Habakkuk, and Zephaniah	Luke	
Ruth and Esther		John	Hebrews
1–2 Samuel		Acts	James
1–2 Kings	Ezekiel	Romans	1–2 Peter and Jude
1–2 Chronicles	Daniel	1 Corinthians	1–3 John
Ezra and Nehemiah	Hosea	2 Corinthians	Revelation
Job	Joel, Amos, and Obadiah	Galatians	

•   •   •   •   •   •

J. I. PACKER is Board of Governors' Professor of Theology at Regent College (Vancouver, BC). Dr. Packer earned his DPhil at the University of Oxford. He is known and loved worldwide as the author of the best-selling book *Knowing God*, as well as many other titles on theology and the Christian life. He serves as the General Editor of the ESV Bible and as the Theological Editor for the *ESV Study Bible*.

LANE T. DENNIS is President of Crossway, a not-for-profit publishing ministry. Dr. Dennis earned his PhD from Northwestern University. He is Chair of the ESV Bible Translation Oversight Committee and Executive Editor of the *ESV Study Bible*.

DANE C. ORTLUND is Executive Vice President of Bible Publishing and Bible Publisher at Crossway. He is a graduate of Covenant Theological Seminary (MDiv, ThM) and Wheaton College (BA, PhD). Dr. Ortlund has authored several books and scholarly articles in the areas of Bible, theology, and Christian living.

NUMBERS

A 12-WEEK STUDY

▲

Michael LeFebvre

∷ CROSSWAY®

WHEATON, ILLINOIS

TABLE OF CONTENTS

▲

SERIES PREFACE

KNOWING THE BIBLE, as the series title indicates, was created to help readers know and understand the meaning, the message, and the God of the Bible. Each volume in the series consists of 12 units that progressively take the reader through a clear, concise study of one or more books of the Bible. In this way, any given volume can fruitfully be used in a 12-week format either in group study, such as in a church-based context, or in individual study. Of course, these 12 studies could be completed in fewer or more than 12 weeks, as convenient, depending on the context in which they are used.

Each study unit gives an overview of the text at hand before digging into it with a series of questions for reflection or discussion. The unit then concludes by highlighting the gospel of grace in each passage ("Gospel Glimpses"), identifying whole-Bible themes that occur in the passage ("Whole-Bible Connections"), and pinpointing Christian doctrines that are affirmed in the passage ("Theological Soundings").

The final component to each unit is a section for reflecting on personal and practical implications from the passage at hand. The layout provides space for recording responses to the questions proposed, and we think readers need to do this to get the full benefit of the exercise. The series also includes definitions of key words. These definitions are indicated by a note number in the text and are found at the end of each chapter.

Lastly, to help understand the Bible in this deeper way, we urge readers to use the ESV Bible and the *ESV Study Bible*, which are available in various print and digital formats, including online editions at esv.org. The *Knowing the Bible* series is also available online.

May the Lord greatly bless your study as you seek to know him through knowing his Word.

J. I. Packer
Lane T. Dennis

Week 1: Overview

Getting Acquainted

Numbers is a book about faithfulness—God's faithfulness even when we are faithless. It is a book about learning from the failures of past generations in order to be more faithful today. Numbers teaches these lessons through the story of two generations of Israel: one generation that consistently breaks faith with God, and an emerging generation that trusts him.

The first generation is introduced with a census (Num. 1:1–4:49), the first of two censuses in the book. This census counts the generation of the exodus who saw God's wonders in Egypt and at Mount Sinai. But in spite of all God's marvels, this first generation is consistently stubborn and rebellious. When God brings them to the border of the Promised Land, their lack of faith hinders them from entering it (13:1–14:45). They are forced to return to the wilderness to wander for another 40 years.

The second generation includes the children raised in those years of wilderness wandering. Their emergence into adulthood is introduced with a second census (26:1–65). This generation learns from their parents' failures and proves faithful to God. They are obedient and quick to repent when corrected—not stiff-necked like their parents were. When this new, faithful generation arrives at the border of the Promised Land, they experience victory and God's blessings (31:1–32:42). Through the experiences of these two generations, we are taught the amazing patience of God despite our faithlessness, and his rich blessings upon those who learn from the past in order to be faithful in the present.

The English title of Numbers is based on the book's organization around two censuses. The Hebrew title of the book is based on a Hebrew word occurring in its first verse, translated "In the wilderness." The entire narrative takes place in Israel's wilderness wanderings from Sinai (1:1) to the "plains of Moab" on the border of Canaan (36:13).

Placing Numbers in the Larger Story

Numbers is the fourth book of the Pentateuch[1] and occupies an important place in the Pentateuch's overarching narrative. Genesis, the first book of the Pentateuch, describes the beginnings of all the nations of the world with a special focus on God's covenant with one house among those nations: the house of Abraham. Exodus continues that narrative with the transformation of Abraham's household through much suffering into a nation redeemed[2] by God and ordered around his law.[3] The book of Leviticus comes next, teaching the gift of atonement[4] at the center of God's kingdom-forming law.

Next, the book of Numbers takes the stage, tracing this newly organized kingdom on its march from Sinai to the border of its promised new land. Numbers assures us of God's faithfulness to his kingdom-building project, even when his people rebel. Deuteronomy concludes the Pentateuch with Moses' final instructions for Israel's settlement in the land, including a vision for taking God's blessings to the rest of the world. The rest of the Bible follows the promises and lessons outlined in the Pentateuch.

Key Verses

"If the LORD delights in us, he will bring us into this land and give it to us, a land that flows with milk and honey. Only do not rebel against the LORD. And do not fear the people of the land, for . . . the LORD is with us" (Num. 14:8–9).

Date and Historical Background

Moses is probably the author of Numbers, writing this and other books of the Pentateuch perhaps during Israel's wilderness wanderings in either the fifteenth or the thirteenth century BC (on the date of the exodus, see page 33 of the *ESV Study Bible*, also available online at www.esv.org). The summary travelogue near the end of Numbers is identified explicitly as written by Moses (33:2). (For further discussion of the date, authorship, and other background material for the book of Numbers, see pages 257–264 in the *ESV Study Bible*, also available online at www.esv.org.)

Outline

I. Lessons from a Faithless Generation (1:1–25:18)

    A. The first census and preparing the camp (1:1–6:27)

    B. Preparing the tabernacle (7:1–10:10)

    C. The need for the right ruler (10:11–12:16)

    D. The need to be a faithful people (13:1–15:41)

    E. The need for the right priesthood (16:1–19:22)

    F. A taste of victory (20:1–21:35)

    G. A faithful God despite a faithless people (22:1–25:18)

II. Lessons from a Faithful Generation (26:1–36:13)

    A. The second census and preparing the camp (26:1–30:16)

    B. A taste of settlement (31:1–32:42)

    C. Review and prospect (33:1–36:13)

As You Get Started

Have you ever read through, studied, or listened to a sermon series on the book of Numbers? What are some of your current highlights or favorite portions of the book, and why?

Read Psalm 78, a sobering review of the "stubborn and rebellious generation" of the exodus, whose story is featured in Numbers. Copy down one or two verses from Psalm 78 that summarize the psalmist's key lessons to watch for in the story of that stubborn generation.

Using a Bible atlas (such as the *ESV Bible Atlas*) or an Internet search engine, review maps and/or photographs of key places in the book of Numbers, such as the Sinai wilderness, Kadesh-barnea, the plains of Moab, and the Jordan River valley. Describe your impressions of the wilderness regions. How would the younger generation feel, after growing up in the wilderness, when they reached the lush fields of Moab and the Jordan River valley?

Did you grow up in a faithful Christian home, or with parents who resisted God's Word? How has your own upbringing prepared you to identify with the blessings and sorrows of the two generations we will meet in the book of Numbers?

> ## As You Finish This Unit . . .

The book of Numbers offers a humbling exposition of our weakness contrasted with a deeply comforting revelation of the Lord's patience, discipline, and restoring grace. As you prepare to begin this study, pray for God to grant you a humble heart to grow in faith as a part of his obedient people.

Definitions

[1] **Pentateuch** – The first five books of the Bible.

[2] **Redemption** – In the context of the Bible, the act of buying back someone who has become enslaved or something that has been lost to someone else. Through his death and resurrection, Jesus purchased redemption for all believers (Col. 1:13–14).

[3] **Law** – When spelled with an initial capital letter, "Law" refers to the first five books of the Bible (see also Pentateuch). The Law contains numerous commands of God to his people, including the Ten Commandments and instructions regarding worship, sacrifice, and life in Israel. The NT often uses "the law" (lower case) to refer to the entire body of precepts set forth in the books of the Law.

[4] **Atonement** – The reconciliation of a person with God, often associated with the offering of a sacrifice. Through his death and resurrection, Jesus Christ made atonement for the sins of believers. His death satisfied God's just wrath against sinful humanity, just as the OT sacrifices symbolized substitutionary death as payment for sin.

Week 2: Preparing the Camp

Numbers 1:1–6:27

▲

The Place of the Passage

The Hebrews left Egypt as freed slaves (Ex. 12:37). At Mount Sinai, the Lord gave them his law and formed them into a new nation (Ex. 19:6; Deut. 33:4–5). Now the time has come to organize them as an army (Num. 1:3, 45) for their march to the Promised Land. These chapters describe the nation's organization as a mobile kingdom, with their King's tent in its midst, as he journeys with his people.

The Big Picture

God does not simply wait for his people at the end of their journey. He meets them in the wilderness to be with them, to guide them, and to bless them on their journey to his Promised Land.

> ## Reflection and Discussion

Read the passages in each section indicated below. Use the provided questions to help you think about the text. Write your thoughts in the space provided, answering the questions and adding further insights. (See notes in the *ESV Study Bible*, pages 265–275; also available online at www.esv.org.)

1. Enrolling the People (1:1–54)

Compare the numbers in this census with the population of Jacob's household when they arrived in Egypt (see Ex. 1:1–7; compare Gen. 22:17). What do we learn about God's goodness in this comparison?

2. Arranging the Camp (2:1–34)

When kings in ancient times led their armies on a campaign, the king's tent was situated in the center of the encampment (e.g., 1 Sam. 26:5). What does the arrangement of Israel's camp indicate (see diagram in the *ESV Study Bible*, page 267)?

The census had been conducted according to the patriarchs' birth order, starting with the tribe of "Reuben, Israel's firstborn" (Num. 1:20). But the order of the tribes' encampment and march places *Judah* at the front (Num. 2:3, 9; note that east, toward the sunrise, was the front in ancient geography). Why would the tribe of Judah lead the way into the land? (See Gen. 49:10; compare 1 Sam. 17:12; Rev. 5:5.)

3. Enrolling the Levites (3:1–4:49)

The tribe of Levi is counted twice. The first count enrolls males one month and older for duties within the camp (3:14–39). The second enrolls males 30 years and older for duties on the march (4:1–49). What are the duties of each Levitical clan in the camp and on the march?

	Inside the Camp (3:14–39)	On the March (4:1–49)
Gershon		
Kohath		
Merari		

4. Consecrating the Camp (5:1–6:21)

The tents of the priests and Levites form the innermost circle around the tabernacle (1:53; 3:21–39). The general population arranges its tents around those of the priests and Levites (1:52; 2:1–34). A third area is now designated for those living under significant impurity (5:1–4). This outermost residence is temporary, lasting only until the impurity is resolved (Lev. 14:1–32; 15:1–33). What do these three concentric bands around the tabernacle, and the purification rituals for moving closer to the tabernacle, teach about God's grace?

After arranging the people's tents in the right places, three laws highlight the importance of strong relationships between tents (5:1–10), within tents

(5:11–31), and toward the center tent (6:1–21). The first (5:1–10) represents relationships between tents. How does the penalty for theft when voluntarily confessed encourage repentance, compared to the penalty when theft is not willingly confessed (Ex. 22:1–4)?

The second law (5:11–31) shows the importance of marital trust. This law is for the protection of a wife when her husband mistreats her under suspicion of her infidelity but without evidence (v. 29). This law provides a way to resolve such baseless jealousy, restoring trust to the marriage. Write here some observations about the symbols of this ceremony.

The third law (the Nazirite vow; 6:1–21) celebrates total consecration to God. Through Nazirite vows, any Israelite could enjoy a temporary status of consecration akin to that of the priests, typically for the purpose of extended worship in God's house. What phrases are used to describe the Nazirite's special status?

5. Benediction (6:22–27)

The section of Numbers about organizing the camp ends with the benediction. What do the three pronouncements of blessing tell us about God's love?

Read through the following three sections on *Gospel Glimpses, Whole-Bible Connections*, and *Theological Soundings*. Then take time to consider the *Personal Implications* of these sections for you.

Gospel Glimpses

DWELLING WITH GOD. It is striking how much space the Pentateuch devotes to the tabernacle.[1] Half of Exodus (25:1–40:38) is spent describing the tabernacle and its construction. Leviticus is devoted to the sacrifices and festivals of the tabernacle. And Numbers emphasizes the place of the tabernacle in the center of the camp. This highly emphasized theme demonstrates the delight of God to dwell *with* his people.

OUTSIDE THE CAMP. The laws in Numbers 5:1–4 require that those with serious conditions of uncleanness[2] be "put out of the camp" (5:2). This instruction is frequently misunderstood as an act of rejection, but it is not. Those placed outside the camp for ritual uncleanness are still identified as members of the camp: it is still called "their camp" in verse 3. Each band of tents around the tabernacle requires a different level of ritual purity depending on its proximity to the sanctuary in the center. The outermost ring is an important part of the overall picture of the gospel presented in the camp's arrangement. Even the most severely impure may attach themselves to the congregation with expectation of cleansing and restoration due to the atonement offered in the tabernacle (see the rituals of cleansing and reincorporation into the camp and the tabernacle in Lev. 12:6–8; 14:1–32; 15:13–15, 28–30).

Whole-Bible Connections

NAZIRITES. Nazirite vows, the rules for which originate in Numbers 6:1–21, are an important theme throughout the Old and New Testaments. Normally, Nazirite vows were undertaken for a limited period of special devotion and worship (e.g., Acts 21:23–26), but there are notable examples of lifelong Nazirites as well. Samson, Samuel, and John the Baptist were lifelong Nazirites. Some suspect that Anna, who "did not depart from the temple, worshiping with fasting and prayer night and day" (Luke 2:37), may also have been a Nazirite in her widowhood.

TENT OF MEETING. The first verse of Numbers begins, "The LORD spoke to Moses in the wilderness of Sinai, *in the tent of meeting.*" This is the first instance of God's meeting with Moses *inside* the tabernacle (although he spoke to Moses *from* the tabernacle on the day of its inauguration; Lev. 1:1). As late as Leviticus 25:1, Moses was still ascending Mount Sinai to meet with the Lord. But Numbers 1:1

introduces the tabernacle in full operation as the "tent of meeting," an important name by which it is known throughout the Bible.

Theological Soundings

PRIESTHOOD OF BELIEVERS. After Jesus completed the final sacrifice, the rituals of Israel's priesthood were to come to an end. This was not because the privileges of priestly worship ended. Rather, in the new covenant all of God's people are a "holy priesthood" (1 Pet. 2:5). The Nazirite vows anticipated this "priesthood of all believers" by providing a way for lay Israelites to undertake a priestly level of ritual purity for a time.

MEDIATION. The priests and Levites encamped between the tabernacle and the other tribes (3:5–10), but they were not there as an obstacle between the people and God. The priests and Levites served as mediators[3] to bring the people acceptably into God's presence (3:8). It is an awesome matter for the holy God to dwell with sinful people. The offices of the priests and Levites represented the need for mediation, fulfilled perfectly in the person and work of the Great High Priest, Jesus Christ (Heb. 12:18–29).

Personal Implications

Consider how your relationship with God is similar to that of the tribes of Israel as illustrated in the arrangement of their camp. Make notes below on personal implications of (1) the *Gospel Glimpses*, (2) the *Whole-Bible Connections*, (3) the *Theological Soundings*, and (4) this passage as a whole.

1. Gospel Glimpses

2. Whole-Bible Connections

3. Theological Soundings

4. Numbers 1:1–6:27

Reflect on the arrangement of the camp described in this passage and consider how this study ought to impact your attitude toward the privilege of worship in God's house. Thank God for assurance of God's presence in your church congregation through Christ, as you journey through life and gather for worship week by week.

Definitions

[1] **Tabernacle** – The tent where God dwelled on earth and communed with his people as Israel's divine King. Also referred to as the "tent of meeting" (Lev. 1:5). The temple in Jerusalem later replaced it.

[2] **Clean/unclean** – The ceremonial, spiritual, or moral state of a person or object, affected by a variety of factors. The terms are primarily related to the concept of holiness and have little to do with actual physical cleanliness. The Mosaic law declared certain foods and animals unclean, and a person became unclean if he or she came in contact with certain substances or objects, such as a dead body. Jesus declared all foods clean (Mark 7:19), and Peter's vision in Acts 10 shows that no person is ceremonially unclean simply because he or she is a Gentile.

[3] **Mediator** – One who intercedes between parties to resolve a conflict or achieve a goal. Jesus is the mediator between God and rebellious humanity (1 Tim. 2:5; compare Heb. 9:15; 12:24).

WEEK 3: PREPARING THE TABERNACLE

Numbers 7:1–10:10

▲

The Place of the Passage

This section introduces a flashback. The tabernacle was set up "on the first day of the first month" (Ex. 40:2, 17). One month later, the census of the people was taken "on the first day of the second month" (Num. 1:1, 18). The people will begin their journey later this same month, on the twentieth day of the second month (10:11). After the report of the census but prior to the departure, Numbers 7:1–10:10 introduces a flashback to something else that took place in the previous month, on "the day when Moses had finished setting up the tabernacle" (7:1; 9:15) and before the census was conducted. This flashback is here because it is important for us to know, before the journey begins, that God's tent is not only set up but is also fully stocked and ready to go. This section describes the stocking and staffing of the tabernacle, its first worship festival, and the glory of God taking up residence there—all of which occur prior to the census (see chart on page 276 of the *ESV Study Bible*).

The Big Picture

The Lord is delighted to take up residence among his people to lead them to the Promised Land.

> ## Reflection and Discussion

Read each of the following sections and use the questions provided to help you think about the blessing of God's presence with his church in every age. (For further insights, see the *ESV Study Bible*, pages 275–281; also available online at www.esv.org.)

1. Stocking and Starting the Tabernacle (7:1–8:4)

On the day the tabernacle is finished, the chiefs of all 12 tribes together bring their initial gift: "six wagons and twelve oxen" (v. 3). What is the purpose of these ox-drawn wagons (vv. 1–9)?

Over 12 days, the chiefs of the 12 tribes each bring an identical contribution, one per day. Each chief's contribution provides for one of every kind of congregational sacrifice. What are the four kinds of congregational offerings each chief provides (e.g., vv. 13, 15, 16, and 17)?

Numbers 7:89–8:4 reports both a literal (God's voice) and a symbolic (the lampstand) demonstration of God's love for the people in response to the chiefs' offerings. What is the significance of these marks of God's blessing occurring at this time?

2. Appointment and Installation of the Levites (8:5–26)

The Levites are inaugurated in a five-part ceremony (vv. 6–7, 8, 9–11, 12, 13). The ceremony's centerpiece occurs when the Levites are presented as the people's "wave offering . . . [to] do the service of the LORD" (vv. 10–11). What is the meaning of their designation as a "wave offering" from the people (vv. 14–19)?

Cleaning, repairing, transporting, and overseeing tabernacle operations is physically demanding work. Guarding the purity of the people for safe entry requires wisdom and tact. How does the division of labor in verses 23–26 reflect these realities?

3. The First Festival (9:1–14)

On the fourteenth day of the first month one year before, the angel of death had passed over Israel's houses to judge Egypt and bring about Israel's redemption. That was the original Passover (Ex. 12:1–32). Now, on the same day one year later, Israel celebrates its first ritual Passover at the newly minted tabernacle (Num. 9:1–5). Consider some of the events that had transpired in the intervening year (especially Ex. 32:1–35) and reflect on how meaningful it would have been to know that Passover redemption was still available. How should this pattern inform our worship week by week and year by year?

On this first tabernacle Passover, several men are unclean because of "touching a dead body" (v. 6). This generally means they had buried a deceased family member. Here are grieving men who need the promises held forth in the Passover but whose ritual impurity bars them from the tabernacle. What do the special provisions in verses 9–14 teach us?

4. Present and Ready to Go! (9:15–10:10)

The event in Numbers 9:15–23 was already reported in Exodus 40:34–38 but is repeated as the crowning purpose of the tabernacle. The God who met with Moses on the mountain will now dwell with the people. What do the seven references to periods of time in verses 19–22 tell us about who sets the cadence for progress on this journey? What does this suggest concerning the life of faith today?

The trumpets used to order the march have a dual purpose. Under what conditions are they used to get the people's attention, and under what conditions do they represent the people's cry for God's attention (10:1–10)?

Read through the following three sections on *Gospel Glimpses*, *Whole-Bible Connections*, and *Theological Soundings*. Then take time to consider the *Personal Implications* these sections may have for you.

Gospel Glimpses

A PROVIDED SACRIFICE. Once the tabernacle is finished, the chiefs of each tribe stock it with sacrifice provisions on behalf of their respective constituencies (7:1–88). It is the chief of the tribe of Judah—the tribe from which the Messiah is anticipated—who leads this ceremony (7:12). These provisions show us that it is the rulers among the people, and especially the chief from Judah, who are held responsible to ensure that the people's atonement is provided for (compare 2 Chron. 35:7). One day, the Messiah would fulfill these patterns by personally providing the final sacrifice[1] for all of his people.

MERCY SEAT. The first divine act in the tabernacle, once it is set up and stocked, is a word spoken "from above the mercy seat" (7:89). The mercy seat is a solid gold plate with golden cherubim, placed on top of the ark (for an artistic conception, see the *ESV Study Bible*, page 184). The ark with the mercy seat is called the "footstool" of God's throne (e.g., 1 Chron. 28:2). God's throne is in heaven, with the ark and its mercy seat as the intersection between heaven and earth (e.g., Isa. 66:1). Hence, to hear the voice of God from over the "mercy seat" is to hear from God's throne in heaven (Ex. 25:17–22). It is through the intercession of Jesus that our personal communion with God, foreshadowed by the mercy seat, is accomplished (Heb. 4:14–16).

Whole-Bible Connections

PASSOVER. The original Passover took place in Egypt (Ex. 12:1–51), but its first ritual celebration is narrated in Numbers 9:1–14. The Passover[2] ritual is one of the most important annual festivals in the biblical narrative. It is during the Passover festival that Jesus is sacrificed as the true Passover lamb (John 19:14). It is also the ritual observance of Passover that is replaced by the New Testament Communion table (Luke 22:14–20).

LEVITES. The term "Levite" occurs 330 times in the Bible (318 times in the Old Testament and 12 times in the New). The role that the members of this tribe serve in the ministries of the tabernacle and the temple can hardly be overemphasized. Their inauguration into that role is reported in Numbers 8:5–26. The Levites are tasked primarily with supervising and guarding the worship at the sanctuary and with teaching God's law to his people.

Theological Soundings

SUBSTITUTION. The Levites are installed into their office in a five-step ceremony (8:5–13). First, they are ritually cleansed (vv. 6–7). Second, they are provided with two bulls for a sacrifice (v. 8). Third, they are presented to the Lord by the congregation (vv. 9–11). Fourth, the two bulls are offered for the Levites' atonement (v. 12). Fifth, the Levites are offered before the priests. The centerpiece of the ceremony is the third step, in which the congregation "shall lay their hands on the Levites" and present them "as a wave offering from the people of Israel" (v. 11). By this process, the Levites are given to God's service "instead of all who open the womb, the firstborn of all the people of Israel. . . . For all the firstborn among the people of Israel are mine" (vv. 16–17). This process teaches the principle of substitution, where one person is accepted by God in the stead of another. Jesus is the ultimate offering whom we the people of God must look to as our substitute.

 Personal Implications

How do the teachings of the Spirit in these passages minister to your faith? Make notes below on personal implications of (1) the *Gospel Glimpses*, (2) the *Whole-Bible Connections*, (3) the *Theological Soundings*, and (4) this passage as a whole.

1. Gospel Glimpses

2. Whole-Bible Connections

3. Theological Soundings

4. Numbers 7:1–10:10

As You Finish This Unit . . .

The Lord has promised, "My word . . . shall not return to me empty, but it shall accomplish that which I purpose" (Isa. 55:11). Pray for the Spirit to fulfill his purposes of grace in your heart through that part of his Word which you have studied in this lesson.

Definitions

[1] **Sacrifice** – An offering to God, often to seek forgiveness of sin. The law of Moses gave detailed instructions regarding various kinds of sacrifices. By his death on the cross, Jesus gave himself as a sacrifice to atone for the sins of believers (Eph. 5:2; Heb. 10:12). Believers are to offer their bodies as living sacrifices to God (Rom. 12:1).

[2] **Passover** – An annual Israelite festival commemorating God's final plague on the Egyptians, which led to the exodus. In this final plague, the Lord "passed over" the houses of those who spread the blood of a lamb on the doorposts of their homes (Exodus 12). Those who did not obey this command suffered the death of their firstborn.

Week 4: The Need for the Right Leader

Numbers 10:11–12:16

▲

The Place of the Passage

The journey finally begins! This passage reports the people's travel from Sinai all the way to the edge of the Promised Land. But on this journey, problems emerge. It is not the terrain or a lack of food that proves problematic but the people's stubbornness toward Moses. Three instances of complaining are reported, each of which highlights the same basic issue: the people need a good shepherd in order to make it through the wilderness.

The Big Picture

God's people need the shepherding care he has appointed.

▶ Reflection and Discussion

Read each of the following sections, introducing the march (10:11–36) and the three complaints that emerge along the way (11:1–3; 11:4–35; 12:1–16). Pause after each section to answer the questions provided. For a map of the likely route of this journey, see the *ESV Study Bible*, page 258, and for more background and notes on the passage, see the *ESV Study Bible*, pages 281–284. (Also available online at www.esv.org.)

1. Off to a Good Start (10:11–36)

When the glory cloud lifts, the people break camp "for the first time" (v. 13). But before leaving, Moses appeals to his brother-in-law Hobab to go with them (vv. 29–32). Moses had married a Cushite woman from a Midianite clan (Ex. 2:16–22; Num. 12:1). What does Moses' speech to her Gentile brother say about the possibility of Gentile adoption into Israel's covenant promises?

2. First Complaint: Misfortunes (11:1–3)

The first complaint story is brief. Note the focus on what the people say in God's hearing, replaced by what Moses says to God as their intercessor. What does this text show us about intercession (compare Rom. 8:34)?

3. Second Complaint: Meat (11:4–35)

In Hebrew, the phrase "our strength is dried up" (v. 6) is "our soul [*nephesh*] is dried up." This idiom refers to how the people lose their appetite for manna. The problem is not a lack of nutrition but a loss of appetite for manna and a "strong craving" (v. 4) for something else. How appetizing do you find the narrator's description of manna (vv. 7–9) compared with the foods from Egypt (vv. 4–6)? What does this say about the Israelites' attitude?

Back when Israel arrived at Sinai, Moses was overwhelmed with the need to adjudicate disputes (Ex. 18:13–27). At that time, tribal judges were enlisted to share Moses' burden as chief judge (Ex. 18:21–22), while Moses continued to be the only teacher for Israel (Ex. 18:20). Now, help in teaching the people is also needed. In Moses' prayer (Num. 11:11–15), which terms capture his emotional anguish for the burden of teaching this vast people alone?

----

4. Third Complaint: Moses (12:1–16)

Even Miriam and Aaron complain about Moses' leadership. In the ancient world, prophecy was often a "family calling," just like royalty, priesthood, and other vocations that also ran in the family (e.g., Num. 18:2). But Moses leads Israel apart from his siblings, and he even married a woman from far outside the family circle. Normally, a prophet would marry a near relation to keep the "family vocation" within the clan. But God defends his exclusive appointment of Moses. What does the Lord identify as unique in his relationship with Moses, which is different from that of any other prophet (Num. 12:6–8)? How does this foreshadow the uniqueness of Christ (Acts 7:37–38)?

All three of the complaints in this series pivot around the leadership of Moses. How has Jesus been revealed as a prophet like Moses (Acts 7:37), yet greater than he (Heb. 3:1–6)?

Read through the following three sections on *Gospel Glimpses, Whole-Bible Connections*, and *Theological Soundings*. Then take time to consider the *Personal Implications* these sections may have for you.

Gospel Glimpses

GRACE. These stories of intercession[1] capture an intriguing irony. On the one hand, it is God who is filled with wrath against the people, and it is Moses who intercedes to pacify that wrath (see 11:1–2). On the other hand, Moses is frustrated with the people and wants to give up. It is God who insists that Moses continue for the sake of the congregation (see 11:10–15). This irony captures beautifully the reality of the gospel. God's wrath is the danger from which we need salvation. But it is also God's grace that provides what is needed for our deliverance. Praise God for such a great salvation!

Whole-Bible Connections

FAITHFUL SERVANT. The New Testament book of Hebrews quotes from this passage, saying, "Consider Jesus . . . who was faithful to him who appointed him, just as Moses also was faithful in all God's house" (Heb. 3:1–2, quoting Num. 12:7). The description "faithful in all God's house" identifies Moses as more than a prophet—he is also a steward in God's house. But "Jesus has been counted worthy of more glory than Moses" (Heb. 3:3). Moses was an exalted *steward* in God's house, "but Christ is faithful over God's house *as a son*" (Heb. 3:6).

KENITES. Moses invites his brother-in-law Hobab to join Israel, promising him a share in the goodness of God to Israel if he does so (10:29–32). The next time we encounter the descendants of Moses' in-laws is in Judges, where Hobab's descendants are known as Kenites: "The descendants of the Kenite, Moses' father-in-law, went up with the people of Judah . . . and settled with the people" (Judg. 1:16). At that time, "Jael, the wife of Heber the Kenite" (Judg. 4:17) saved Israel from the Canaanites by slaying Sisera (Judg. 4:12–24; 5:24–27). So we see the family of Hobab going from complete outsiders in Numbers to those who provide a savior for God's people in Judges. This is a glorious picture of the richness and width of God's saving purposes for the world.

▶ Theological Soundings

MEEKNESS. In traditional honor-shame societies, meekness is regarded as a sign of weakness. According to customary principles of honor and shame, when a leader's honor is challenged, he must defend his honor or risk losing it to the challenger. Honor is viewed as a commodity to be either defended or lost. However, Moses embodies a different model of leadership that establishes a different standard for God's people: "Now the man Moses was very meek, more than all people who were on the face of the earth" (Num. 12:3). Moses does not seek to preserve his own glory but humbly leaves his reputation in God's hands. Thus the trait of meekness is esteemed as a virtue among the people of God (compare Matt. 5:5, 39; Mark 15:5).

ELDERS. The tribes of Israel had elders[2] long before their ordination by Moses. Moses' ordination of the elders (Num. 11:16–30) is not the beginning of elders in Israel but is the beginning of their organization as undershepherds teaching God's Word as revealed through Moses. The elders had previously served as community heads, each representing his own clan. (There were 70 clans among the 12 tribes; compare 26:1–65.) God tells Moses to gather the 70 elders from all of Israel's clans, "whom you know to be the elders of the people [i.e., who are already their elders]," and "I will take some of the Spirit that is on you and put it on them, and they shall bear the burden of the people with you" (11:16–17). The key feature of that announcement is the phrase "with you." Henceforward, the elders will serve no longer merely as community leaders but as undershepherds extending the spiritual leadership of Moses. It is this vocation of spiritual eldership that continues to be the backbone of the shepherding of Jesus through his church (1 Tim. 3:1–7; 1 Pet. 5:1–5).

SONG. Two short statements are repeated by Moses each time the ark moves or comes to a point of rest (Num. 10:35–36). These may be songs that are sung. Every time the ark is lifted to begin a new leg of their journey, Moses says (or sings), "Arise, O LORD, and let your enemies be scattered, and let those who hate you flee before you." Whenever the ark is placed at a new stopping point, Moses says (or sings), "Return, O LORD, to the ten thousand thousands of Israel." These are probably the first lines of songs that Moses sings on these occasions (compare Pss. 68:1; 132:8). Throughout the Bible, singing is an important tool of faith both in worship and within the various life events of God's people. Song is not simply a means for entertainment; in fact, it is probably only in recent centuries that music has become regarded as primarily an entertainment art. Historically, music has served as a tool of social unity as well as of sharing and shaping beliefs. The songs of the ark contribute to the biblical theology of song and our understanding of the ark's role and significance.

Personal Implications

Make notes below on personal implications of (1) the *Gospel Glimpses*, (2) the *Whole-Bible Connections*, and (3) the *Theological Soundings* from your study in this passage, as well as any remarks on (4) this passage as a whole.

1. Gospel Glimpses

2. Whole-Bible Connections

3. Theological Soundings

4. Numbers 10:11–12:16

As You Finish This Unit . . .

In this passage, we have been reminded of our need for a Good Shepherd to lead the people through the wilderness. As an aid in responding to this study, read or sing Psalm 23 and praise God for the Good Shepherd he has provided in Christ Jesus, asking for grace to reverence his instruction to us.

Definitions

[1] **Intercession** – Appealing to one person on behalf of another. Often used with reference to prayer.

[2] **Elder** – A recognized leader charged with oversight of a community or organized body. In the NT, an officer in the local church (Acts 14:23; 1 Tim. 3:1–7) charged primarily with spiritual oversight.

WEEK 5: THE NEED TO BE A FAITHFUL PEOPLE

Numbers 13:1–15:41

The Place of the Passage

The book of Numbers might have ended at this point if the people had trusted God and entered the land at his command. Instead, rebellion brings an extra 40 years of wanderings. It is the people's rebellion at this center point in the book that introduces one of the greatest surprises of the Old Testament. The exodus from Egypt is the preeminent Old Testament example of God's redemption; yet, the very same generation that experienced the exodus becomes the preeminent Old Testament example of stubbornness (e.g., Ps. 78:5–8). How can it be that those who have seen the great works of God's salvation are so hard-hearted (see Num. 14:11)? This passage is a turning point in the book and a crucial witness to all believers who follow after, "that they should not be like their fathers, a stubborn and rebellious generation" (Ps. 78:8).

The Big Picture

Rebellion results not from a lack of evidence that God is good but from an unwillingness to trust in his goodness.

▶ Reflection and Discussion

This passage is divided into three sections. Read each portion of Scripture in turn, using the space provided to write your notes on the questions provided. (For further notes on the text, see the *ESV Study Bible*, pages 285–290; also at www.esv.org.)

1. A Bad Report (13:1–14:10)

The spies' mission is not a feasibility study. The Lord makes his promise clear (13:2): this survey is to bring back encouragement ("be of good courage"; 13:20) concerning the land. What evidence of the land's goodness do the scouts find? (For a map of the spies' likely route, see the *ESV Study Bible*, page 286.)

The plea of Moses, Aaron, Caleb, and Joshua is inspired by their confidence that "the LORD is with us" (14:9). What are some of the tangible lessons—both in past deeds and in camp arrangements—that the people now deny?

2. A Sad Result (14:11–45)

It would have been good if the people had heeded Moses' appeals to repent before the Lord appeared. The people do repent *after* God appears in his glory, and God does forgive them (v. 20). But their calling changes. They are now called to serve as another generation of waiting instead of becoming the generation to receive the land (vv. 21–24). What should we learn about the nature of repentance and forgiveness from this example?

The people justified their rebellion based on love for their children (v. 3). In reality, their rebellion brings prolonged suffering upon their children (v. 33). In what other ways does their punishment fit the crime (compare vv. 2 and 28–29; vv. 3 and 43–45; vv. 10 and 37–38)?

---

3. Rituals of Faith (15:1–41)

What could be more beautiful, after being sent back into the wilderness, than the opening words of chapter 15: "Speak to the people of Israel and say to them, 'When you come into the land you are to inhabit, which I am giving you . . .'" (v. 2)? A chapter of sacrifice laws might seem dull to modern readers, but these laws allow the Israelites in the wilderness to anticipate the day their children will harvest Canaan's bounty and present these offerings. Note some phrases in verses 1–21 that stir visions of the land.

Laws about forgiveness (vv. 22–31) add further comfort. The Hebrew verb translated "sin unintentionally" means literally "to commit a sin of wandering," as when a sheep wanders from its shepherd (compare Ezek. 34:6). Sins of wandering are those committed by one whose desire is to be right with God but who is led astray by deception or who falls through weakness or sins in ignorance (i.e., "unintentionally"). Sins committed "with a high hand" are those committed in frank defiance. These were atoned for not through the regular sacrifices but only on the Day of Atonement (Lev. 16:16). How should Old Testament laws like these inform the way we view our own sins, with some being more severe than others but all finding atonement through Christ?

The narrative of the man "gathering sticks on the Sabbath day" (vv. 32–36) illustrates one "who does anything with a high hand" and who thus "reviles the Lord" (vv. 30–31). Violating the Sabbath did not generally require execution (Ezek. 20:12–24; Jer. 17:19–27; Neh. 13:15–21), but this is a case of high-handed defiance, performing an otherwise innocent activity (gathering sticks) in deliberate mockery of God's Sabbath. Read Deuteronomy 5:12–15 and discuss what promises the Sabbath has been appointed to remember, which this man's deliberate mockery of the day repudiates.

Read through the following three sections on *Gospel Glimpses, Whole-Bible Connections,* and *Theological Soundings.* Then take time to consider the *Personal Implications* these sections may have for you.

▶ Gospel Glimpses

YAHWEH SAVES. When Moses selects men to spy out the land, each is a "chief" from his respective tribe (13:2). This is not a military deployment but a selection of leaders who would be able to inspire the people through their reports of the land's goodness. Their mission is one of encouragement, not advanced conquest. The lead member of the expedition is a chief from the tribe of Ephraim named

Hoshea, whose name means "he saves." Moses changes his name to Joshua (Yah + Hoshea), giving the revised meaning, "Yahweh[1] saves" (13:16). It is Yahweh whose salvation will bring his people to their new home. (Notably, the name "Jesus" is the Greek version of Joshua.)

Whole-Bible Connections

MILK AND HONEY. The spies characterize the Promised Land as a land of "milk and honey" (13:27; 14:8). This phrase becomes a stock description for Canaan's bounty. Milk (particularly its cream) was a luxury product from livestock farming. Honey was a luxury product from farming the land. It refers not to bee honey but to a sweet paste made from figs, dates, or even grapes (Gen. 43:11; 2 Kings 18:32; Ezek. 27:17). Sometimes, the same term is used also for the sweet product of bees, but ancient Hebrews did not keep bees. They enjoyed honey from beehives only when they found it in the wild (Deut. 32:13; Judges 14:8). As a phrase for possessing and farming the land, the expression "milk and honey" represents the pleasures enjoyed from an idyllic land for keeping livestock as well as crops and orchards; it is a foretaste of the glorious pleasure of our future promised land, the new heavens and the new earth, in which we will dwell with the Lord forever.

Theological Soundings

FAITH. All 12 spies encounter the same evidence. But the 10 doubting spies let that evidence alone form their conclusions about God's ability to give them the land, and they doubt. Caleb and Joshua allow their knowledge of God from his past deeds (e.g., the exodus from Egypt) to form the basis of their conclusions about the evidence they encounter in Canaan. (Compare 13:31 and 13:30; 14:9.) The heart of doubt needs to re-prove God's trustworthiness with every trial (14:11). The heart of faith is able to rest in the great goodness of God abundantly demonstrated already, framing each new trial by what is already known of God's faithfulness (compare Pss. 78, especially vv. 7, 11, 22, 32; 95:8–11; also David's perspective on Goliath versus that of his brothers in 1 Samuel 17).

FORGIVENESS. In his prayer, Moses quotes a catechism-like statement found frequently in the Old Testament: "The LORD is slow to anger and abounding in steadfast love, forgiving iniquity and transgression, but he will by no means clear the guilty, visiting the iniquity of the fathers on the children, to the third and fourth generation" (14:18; compare Ex. 20:5–6; 34:6–7; Deut. 5:9–10; Pss. 86:15; 103:7–18; Joel 1:3). This statement reminds us that God is full of grace and quick to forgive those who repent but that he will "by no means" ignore sin.[2] There must be repentance, not only for the sake of the sinner but also for the sake of his or her household. The phrase "third and fourth generation" represents the members of a typical Hebrew household. The idolatry of a head of household has consequences for his children and grandchildren (and sometimes great-grandchildren) who grow up in such an idolatrous household. This catechetical statement captures a sobering reality, but it does not mean that children are judged for a parent's sins. When children abandon the sins of parents, there is full forgiveness (Ex. 20:5–6; Ezek. 18:1–32), as illustrated by the second generation in the book of Numbers.

Personal Implications

Take time to reflect on the lessons on atonement symbolized in the offerings in Leviticus 1:1–6:7 as they minister to your own faith today. Make notes below on personal implications of (1) the *Gospel Glimpses*, (2) the *Whole-Bible Connections*, (3) the *Theological Soundings*, and (4) this passage as a whole.

1. Gospel Glimpses

2. Whole-Bible Connections

3. Theological Soundings

4. Numbers 13:1–15:41

As You Finish This Unit . . .

This passage confronts our tendency to wander like sheep, or even to defy God with a "high hand." Examine your own heart and confess your sin, looking to the sacrifice of Christ as your only hope for forgiveness and acceptance by God. Then give him thanks, and rededicate yourself to serve him and to encourage others in faith.

Definitions

[1] **Yahweh** – The likely English form of the name represented by the Hebrew letters YHWH. The Lord revealed this unique name for himself to Moses at the burning bush and told him to instruct the Israelites to call on him by this name (Exodus 3). English translations of the Bible usually render this term as "LORD," with small capital letters. (YHWH can also be translated "GOD," in small capitals.)

[2] **Sin** – Any violation of or failure to adhere to the commands of God, or the desire to do so.

WEEK 6: THE NEED FOR THE RIGHT PRIESTHOOD

Numbers 16:1–19:22

▲

The book of Numbers has previously highlighted the need for the right ruler (Moses) to lead the people's journey (10:11–12:16). In the present passage, we learn of the people's need for the right priest (Aaron) to intercede for their atonement (13:1–15:41). Sadly, as with many lessons in Numbers, these lessons are taught through the failures of the exodus generation. But against the backdrop of their rebellion against the priesthood of Aaron, God's grace shines brightly in giving us Jesus as the perfect successor to Aaron's priesthood. Despite the people's resistance, God persists in upholding the priesthood that ministers salvation to them—and, through Jesus, to us.

The Big Picture

God's people need the priestly intercession he has appointed, which is foreshadowed in Aaron and the Levites and completed by Jesus.

Reflection and Discussion

This passage includes two narratives and two blocks of law related to the theme of the priesthood. Read each section and use the provided questions to help you think about the text. (For additional perspective, see the *ESV Study Bible*, pages 291–296; also available online at org.)

1. Korah's Rebellion (16:1–50)

Korah is a Levite who seeks to be Israel's high priest instead of Aaron. Dathan, Abiram, and On are leaders among the Reubenites who back Korah's attempted coup. Korah also gains support from 250 other Levites who want to be priests too. They accuse Moses and Aaron of "exalt[ing] yourselves" (v. 3), but who is the actual subject of their attack (vv. 5, 7, 11)? What does this tell us about their hearts?

Moses proposes a test whereby God would reveal his choice of who would be the high priest. One of the privileges of the priest was to take coals from the sacrifice altar to burn incense and offer prayers on behalf of the people. The next morning, Korah and his 250 would attempt that priestly duty alongside Aaron to see which man God receives as the people's priest. Why is it particularly egregious that Levites are the ones seeking priestly status (v. 9)?

The Reubenite rebels (with Dathan) show disdain for Moses as "prince" (v. 13) by refusing his summons (vv. 12–15), while the Levite rebels (with Korah) show disdain for Aaron's priesthood by coming with their own incense censers

(vv. 16–19). Who else stands with Korah and his pseudo-priests for morning prayers that day (v. 19a)? What will it mean for the people if they approach God behind the wrong priests?

God tells Moses and Aaron he will destroy the congregation (vv. 20–21). But, like true intercessors, Moses and Aaron plead for mercy and urge the people to separate from the rebels. All of the people do so except (sadly) the families of Korah, Dathan, and Abiram. What features of the disaster that follows make it clear that the judgment is from the Lord?

How do the actions of Aaron the next day demonstrate the benefits a grumbling people receive when their priest loves them and uses his own acceptance before God to intercede for them (vv. 41–50)? How does this foreshadow the work of Jesus?

2. A Lasting Testimony (17:1–13)

What is the significance of the sign God provides—the blossoming of a dead stick—to seal his choice of Aaron as high priest? How do you think this sign might address specifically the people's fears about approaching God in worship (vv. 12–13)?

Two tangible memorials serve to remind Israel of the events that sealed God's choice of Aaron's house as the priestly line. What is the particular reminder of the bronze cover over the altar for anyone who approaches the altar to collect coals for incense (16:36–40)? What is the particular reminder attached to Aaron's staff kept in the tabernacle (17:1–13)?

3. Supporting the Priests (18:1–32)

This section contains laws about financing the priests (vv. 8–20) and the Levites (vv. 21–32). The other eleven tribes will receive land from which to produce farms and businesses. The priests and Levites, however, are restricted from engaging in economic ventures (vv. 20, 24), so God promises to pay for their livelihood from the offerings the people bring to him. List some of the key phrases from Numbers 18:1–32 that repeatedly indicate that it is God (not the people) who will support the priests and Levites.

4. A Priestly "Cleanser" (19:1–22)

God's people need a priest who atones for their sins. They also need a priest who provides cleansing from the stains of sin. That is what this final block of laws is about. The book of Leviticus makes a distinction between sins (like stealing, lust, and bitterness) and the stains of sin (like disease and death; Lev. 10:10). To die is not a sin, but death is a consequence of our sinful condition (Gen. 3:19). In order for God to dwell in a camp filled with both sin and its stains, the people need priests who will atone for their sin and will also provide rituals of cleansing from its stains. The ashes of the red heifer, maintained and applied by the priests, represents such cleansing. When these rituals of cleansing are not observed, what becomes defiled by the lack of cleansing (Num. 19:13, 20)? What does this teach us about God's grace in the face of human suffering and death?

Read through the following three sections on *Gospel Glimpses*, *Whole-Bible Connections*, and *Theological Soundings*. Then take time to consider the *Personal Implications* these sections may have for you.

 ## Gospel Glimpses

NEW LIFE. There is much fearful judgment and death in this section of Numbers. It is no wonder the people cry out to Moses, "Everyone who comes near, who comes near to the tabernacle of the LORD, shall die. Are we all to perish?" (17:13). But the danger of sinful men and women approaching the presence of a holy God is only half the story. God also provides a stunning promise of life in his presence through the miraculous sprouting of Aaron's rod (17:1–13). By this miracle, the Lord shows that there is not death but eternal life[1] and joy for those who approach him through his chosen priest.

 ## Whole-Bible Connections

KORAH AND DATHAN. The rebellion of Korah and Dathan became legendary in Israel (Deut. 11:6; Ps. 106:16–17; Jude 11). Korah is the "son of Izhar, son of Kohath, son of Levi" (16:1), making him Aaron's first cousin (compare Ex. 6:18, 21). In other words, Korah is about as close to the priestly line as possible without being part of it. Dathan and his collaborators are chiefs in the tribe of

Reuben (16:1). Reuben was the firstborn among the 12 patriarchs, and normally leadership would remain in the firstborn's lineage. Dathan, as a natural heir to leadership in Israel, is jealous that Moses possesses that status as Israel's "prince" (16:13). Both Korah and Dathan have natural reasons to be jealous of the roles of Moses and Aaron. Nevertheless, it is God who gives his people the mediator(s) he has chosen. The rebellion of Korah and Dathan serves as an abiding reminder to submit to the Lord's chosen priest and prince for his people, roles filled ultimately by Jesus.

Theological Soundings

TITHES AND OFFERINGS. Numbers 18:1–32 is the most extensive passage in the Bible describing the Old Testament system of support for temple officers. The key principle to note in this chapter is its repeated emphasis that God is the one who will support the priests and Levites. It is not the people who will pay their salaries. The people bring their due tithes and offerings as gifts of worship to God, but it is the Lord who pays the priests and Levites from those resources to support their labors. By this method of support, the priests and Levites are to be free to devote their energies to their ministry and are not to become entangled in farming or trade or other economic pursuits. Furthermore, by this method of support it is made clear that God is the one who supports the temple as his gift for the good of the people, not the other way around. Although the kinds of tithes and offerings brought in the New Testament church are different from the altar sacrifices brought in the temple, Paul teaches us that the same principle continues for the support of ministers in the New Testament church: "Do you not know that those who are employed in the temple service get their food from the temple? . . . In the same way, the Lord commanded that those who proclaim the gospel should get their living by the gospel" (1 Cor. 9:13–14).

PRAYER. It is truly an awesome thing to have an audience with the holy God! The judgment on Korah and his associates reminds us of how dangerous prayer would be apart from a divinely approved intercessor. This judgment teaches us never to approach God in any other name than that of the intercessor he has given to us. It is now Christ who has undertaken the office of Great High Priest, and it is in his name that we have ready and gracious access to heaven (Heb. 4:14–5:6).

Personal Implications

Make notes below on personal implications of (1) the *Gospel Glimpses*, (2) the *Whole-Bible Connections*, (3) the *Theological Soundings*, and (4) this passage as a whole.

1. Gospel Glimpses

2. Whole-Bible Connections

3. Theological Soundings

4. Numbers 16:1–19:22

As You Finish This Unit . . .

Read Hebrews 8:1–6, and close this study with prayer thanking the Father for the perfect mediation of our King Jesus as well as his perfect intercession as our Great High Priest.

Definitions

[1] **Eternal life** – For believers, the new life that begins with trust in Jesus Christ alone for salvation and that continues after physical death with an eternity in God's presence in heaven.

Week 7: A Taste of Victory

Numbers 20:1–21:35

▲

This passage begins "in the first month" (20:1) of a new year. The text does not state which year this is, but it is probably the start of the fortieth year, as this passage reports the final march of the people to their last encampment on the edge of the Promised Land (compare Num. 20:22–29 with 33:38). With the events of this passage, the people's wanderings end as they reach Canaan's border. As they approach the land, the people experience their first taste of warfare—and their first victories. Notwithstanding these early victories won by the hand of the Lord, the exodus generation is as full of complaints as ever, as we approach the end of that generation. Few books of the Bible showcase the patience of God so beautifully as Numbers, which sets his stubborn faithfulness against the people's stubborn faithlessness.

The Big Picture

Despite real losses due to the people's faithlessness, the Lord continues to be faithful and advances his purposes for them with great victories.

▶ Reflection and Discussion

This passage concludes the people's journeys, bringing them to the border of Canaan, where they set up camp for the last time. Carefully follow these final events of their wanderings, reading each section below and writing your thoughts after each of the provided prompts. (For further assistance as you consider these verses, see the notes in the *ESV Study Bible*, pages 296–301; also online at www.esv.org.)

1. The Eclipse of Miriam, Moses, and Aaron (20:1–29)

Miriam's death is reported at the beginning of chapter 20 (v. 1), and Aaron's death is reported at its end (vv. 22–29). Furthermore, Moses will not be permitted to enter the land (v. 12). A transition between generations is taking place. But the people's complaining at the end of their wanderings is just like it was at the beginning (compare Ex. 15:22–17:7; Num. 11:4–9). What is it about Moses' response to this instance of the people's complaining that will keep him from leading them into the land? (Compare Ps. 106:32–33.)

For their failure, Moses and Aaron are told they will die in the wilderness (v. 12). It might seem unfair for this singular failure to bar them from leading the people into the land, but what does this tell us about the standard of perfection that must be met by a mediator who would successfully lead God's people into his rest?

Edom refuses Israel passage through its territory, resulting in a roundabout march (see map on page 296 of the *ESV Study Bible*.) Why does Moses introduce

Israel to Edom as "your brother Israel" (v. 14)? Why does he expect Edom to take interest in Israel's story and allow them passage? (See Gen. 36:1–8.)

God takes Aaron from the people, but he does not take away the high priesthood. Note that Israel's first succession of high priests takes place not in the tabernacle but on a high mountain (20:22–29). What do you suppose this represents about the high priesthood? (For the high priest's vestments, see Exodus 28 and 39 and the depiction on page 208 of the *ESV Study Bible*.)

2. First Conflicts and Victories (21:1–35)

The attack of the king of Arad is Israel's first confrontation with the Canaanites as they re-approach the border (v. 1). Why is the result of this confrontation at the place called Hormah (v. 3) different from the previous time Israel confronted Canaanites at the place called Hormah (see Num. 14:39–45)?

A repeated theme through the story of the exodus generation has been their complaining about the manna God has given them. As we approach the end of this generation's history, Numbers 21:4–9 records one final complaint about "this worthless food" (v. 5), and it has a surprising end: this time, the people actually repent (v. 7)! God grants healing for those who repent, with a tangible reminder of his eagerness to forgive: a bronze serpent (vv. 4–9). Read John 3:14–17 and discuss how the bronze serpent foreshadows Christ.

Israel is not authorized to attack non-Canaanites, for only the Canaanites are under God's judgment. How does Israel's varied responses to Edom, Arad, the Amorites, and the Bashanites illustrate Israel's carefulness to limit conflict to God's commandment? Fill in "Israel's Response" in the spaces provided in the table below. (For a map of these kingdoms, see the ESV *Study Bible*, page 300.)

	Character of Confrontation	Israel's Response
Edom (20:20–21) (Non-Canaanite)	Edom refuses Israel's offer of peace and threatens but does not attack.	
Arad (21:1–3) (Canaanite)	Arad attacks and takes captives.	(See note on 21:2–3 in the ESV *Study Bible*, page 298.)
Amorites (21:21–32) (Non-Canaanite)	The Amorites refuse Israel's offer of peace, attacking them instead.	
Bashanites (21:33–35) (Non-Canaanite)	As Israel passes by, the Bashanites send out armies to attack them.	

In the middle of narrating these conflicts, Numbers 21:10–20 reports a well Israel digs in an uninhabited region of "no man's land" between the Amorites and the Moabites (v. 13). How does this peaceful development of making unclaimed wilderness habitable contribute to the "taste" of settling the land that the exodus generation receives on the borders of Canaan?

The exodus generation is not permitted to enter the land, but they receive a foretaste of the victories their children will experience in it. Read through the following three sections on *Gospel Glimpses*, *Whole-Bible Connections*, and *Theological Soundings*, then take time to consider the *Personal Implications* these sections have for your faith and sanctification.

 ## Gospel Glimpses

BRONZE SERPENT. John 3:16 is one of the most familiar verses in the Bible: "For God so loved the world, that he gave his only Son, that whoever believes in him should not perish but have eternal life." But have you ever noticed that Jesus makes this statement to explain the significance of the bronze serpent in Numbers 21:4–9? In John 3:14–15, Jesus retells the bronze serpent event and then in verse 16 adds his "for" statement to explain how the bronze serpent was a type[1] of himself. The "so" in John 3:16 does not mean "so much" but rather "in this way," further drawing a parallel between the bronze serpent and Jesus' work on the cross. The bronze serpent was raised up for the people who were dying in their sins. They looked in repentance and received life. So it is with those who trust in the cross of Christ.

Whole-Bible Connections

EDOM. Edom, located on the southeast border of Israel, shares a relationship to Israel that spans nearly the entire Bible. The Edomites originated from the offspring of Esau when he separated from Jacob (Gen. 36:6–8). It is their parentage in Isaac's twin sons—Israel descending from Jacob and Edom from Esau—that leads to their frequent depiction as "brother" nations (Num. 20:14; Deut. 23:7; Obad. 10; Mal. 1:2). But, like Jacob and Esau, their brotherhood is one of rivalry (1 Sam. 14:47; 22:9; 2 Sam. 8:14; 1 Kings 11:14–16; 2 Kings 3:9; 8:20). When the Babylonians invade Judah in the sixth century BC, the Edomites participate in the devastation of Jerusalem (Ps. 137:7; Obad. 10–14). By the time of Jesus' birth, Herod the Great is reigning over Israel. The Bible records little about Herod's lineage, but extrabiblical evidence indicates he is probably an Idumean (Idumea being the name at that time for Edom). In spite of this tumultuous history, Jesus welcomes the crowds that come to hear him "from Galilee and Judea and Jerusalem *and Idumea* and from beyond the Jordan and from around Tyre and Sidon" (Mark 3:7–8).

Theological Soundings

JUST WAR AND HOLY WAR. Far too often, religion has been used as a pretext for war. Israel's conquests in Canaan have sometimes been misused to justify such warfare. However, attention to the text reveals a careful distinction between true "holy war" and other forms of war. During the days of Abraham, God's people lived at peace among the Canaanites, even engaging in business and military alliances with them (e.g., Gen. 14:1–24; 21:25–32). God had not authorized judgment upon Canaan, "for the iniquity of the Amorites [was] not yet complete" (Gen. 15:16). Then, four centuries later, the divine Judge did declare final judgment exclusively upon Canaan (Deut. 9:4–5). The term "holy war" should be used only for an actual decree from heaven pronouncing judgment[2] on a people. Israel's authorization for holy war was strictly limited to the peoples of Canaan. All other enemies were to be approached with "terms of peace" (Deut. 20:1–20). Other wars might be fought defensively (i.e., a "just war") but not merely for conquest. The battles in Numbers 20:14–21; 21:1–3, 21–35 are carefully described to show the divine judgment visited upon *Canaanite* Arad in contrast with efforts to maintain peace with the non-Canaanite nations of Edom, the Amorites, and Bashan. The latter two are defeated in what Numbers describes specifically as defensive warfare. In Judges 11:12–28, Jephthah again stresses the defensive posture of Israel's warfare that results in their possessing land east of the Jordan, outside of Canaan. The conquest of Canaan is a foreshadowing of the final judgment that one day will purge the whole world of sin in order to make the land a dwelling place for righteousness. But the Canaanite conquest cannot be used to justify human leaders' initiating religiously motivated violence.

Personal Implications

Take time to reflect on the lessons on faith, holiness, and judgment in this week's study. In the space below, make notes on your personal responses to (1) the *Gospel Glimpses*, (2) the *Whole-Bible Connections*, (3) the *Theological Soundings*, and (4) this passage as a whole.

1. Gospel Glimpses

2. Whole-Bible Connections

3. Theological Soundings

4. Numbers 20:1–21:35

As You Finish This Unit . . .

Although the stories vary and many new lessons emerge with each section of the book, the overarching message of Numbers is one of assurance concerning God's faithfulness and of exhortation to repent of our own faithlessness. As we approach the final episode of the faithless exodus generation, pray for God to use this study in Numbers to open your heart to grow in faithfulness.

Definitions

[1] **Typology** – A method of interpretation in which a real, historical object, place, or person is recognized as a pattern or foreshadowing (a "type") of some later object, place, or person. For example, the Bible presents Adam as a "type" of Christ (Rom. 5:14).

[2] **Judgment** – Any assessment of something or someone, especially moral assessment. The Bible also speaks of a final day of judgment when Christ returns, when all those who have refused to repent will be judged (Rev. 20:12–15).

WEEK 8: A FINAL TEST OF FAITHFULNESS

Numbers 22:1–25:18

▲

The Place of the Passage

This is the final episode of the exodus generation, as the new generation emerges into leadership in the next section (Num. 26:1–65). In this concluding episode of the exodus generation, Moab (one of the remaining nations east of the Jordan) tries to destroy Israel. Moab's first attempt is to hire a seer, Balaam, to curse Israel. However, God turns Balaam's curses into blessings for his people (22:1–24:25). Moab tries a second time, this time tempting Israel directly with adulterous worship of Baal. This is Israel's first encounter with this Canaanite deity, and tragically the Israelites quickly surrender to the allure of Baal worship (25:1–18). No pair of events captures the stunning goodness of God, on the one hand, and the equally stunning faithlessness of the exodus generation, on the other, as vividly as these capstone events from that generation.

The Big Picture

God's people enjoy his unconditional love yet are easily distracted by the temptations of idolatry.

> **Reflection and Discussion**

Read each part of the passage as outlined below, answering the provided questions and noting other related thoughts. (See the notes in the *ESV Study Bible*, pages 301–307, for further prompts and insights as you read; also online at www.esv.org.)

1. Moab Summons Balaam (22:1–41)

The attempts of other kings to stop Israel have failed. The king of Moab, in consultation with Midianite elders in his lands, determines that Israel must be weakened before Moab can attempt an attack. In order to defeat Israel in battle, Moab must first compromise Israel's true source of strength (22:1–6). What does Balak's strategy teach us about the true source of Israel's success?

In verses 7–21, Moab's delegation presses Balaam to come with them, but God will not allow it. Tempted by promises of wealth, Balaam seeks to persuade God to let him go (compare 2 Pet. 2:15; Jude 11). What indications of Balaam's greed and his efforts to prevail upon God do you note in the passage?

God finally accedes to Balaam's pleas to go but still holds him responsible for his sinful greed (Num. 22:20, 22). Compare this event to the occasion in which Israel lusted for meat and God relented to the request but did not excuse the people's sin (11:18–20, 33). How do these lessons teach us about the ways of

God at times in which we stubbornly pursue our sins and he seems to allow us what we want?

The story of Balaam and his donkey is one of the most humorous in the Bible. However, its irony is here not to entertain but to reveal profound lessons about the seer who cannot see (v. 33), the God who can speak by whomever he pleases (v. 28), and the honor-seeking man who is exposed as a fool (v. 29). What key lesson does Balaam learn through his donkey before he arrives in Moab (compare vv. 20, 35, and 38)?

---

2. Curses Turned to Blessings (23:1–24:13)

By strictly constraining Balaam to speak only as instructed, God turned the curses of Balaam into blessings for his people (compare Josh. 24:9–10; Neh. 13:2). Balaam attempts to curse three times, with each instance resulting in blessing instead. Which elements of Balaam's three oracles[1] are particularly comforting to you?

Balaam yearns for the wealth Balak offers but is unable to do what is required to receive it. Whom did both Balak and Balaam blame for the failure of their collaborative effort (24:10–13)?

---

3. Blessings Turned to Curses (24:14–25)

Balaam finally announces a curse—against Israel's enemies! Moab's plan to curse Israel backfires. How does this turn of events demonstrate God's promise to Abraham in Genesis 12:2–3?

Balaam's final oracle anticipates the fall of Israel's enemies (such as Moab, Edom, and Amalek), the future rise of the Assyrian Empire (Asshur; v. 22), and the eventual fall of the Assyrians before invaders from Kittim (Greece; v. 24). But the highlight of this final oracle is the vision in verse 17: who or what is promised in this verse?

---

4. Israel's First Encounter with Baal (25:1–18)

Having failed to remove God's blessing from Israel, Moab and the Midianite elders try a different approach. They seek to allure Israel to abandon God's blessing. Sadly, the people are quick to join the Moabite fertility cult, yoking themselves to Baal (v. 3). Israel's chiefs begin to marry the daughters of Moabite and Midianite chiefs (hence the expression "brought a Midianite woman to his family"; vv. 6, 14–15). What does the adulterous character of Israel's first sin with Baal indicate about the nature of all idolatry, in God's eyes? (Note the self-description of God in v. 11.)

All of Israel's chiefs deserve to perish, and a plague breaks out against all Israel (vv. 4–5, 8–9). But God stops the plague when the people repent (v. 6), and a judge in Israel brings justice against one representative ringleader (vv. 5, 11). How does this illustrate God's eagerness to atone for his people when they repent (v. 13), contrasted with the full justice visited upon those outside his covenant (vv. 17–18)?

Those who perish in the plague include the last members of the exodus generation (25:9; 26:64). As we come to the end of the generation that experienced God's miracles in Egypt and his care through the wilderness (Exodus 1:1–Numbers 25:18), review Psalm 78 and identify one or two key lessons that this psalm helps us to learn from that "stubborn and rebellious generation" (Ps. 78:8).

Read through the following three sections on *Gospel Glimpses*, *Whole-Bible Connections*, and *Theological Soundings*. Then take time to consider the *Personal Implications* these sections may have for you.

Gospel Glimpses

UNCONDITIONAL LOVE. Remarkably, throughout the Balaam narrative there is no indication that Israel knows what is happening. The account seems to indicate that Balak hires Balaam and engages in repeated efforts to curse Israel but that Israel knows nothing about it. Israel learns about Balaam's efforts after the fact (see Num. 31:8, 16), but God's love is at work even when Israel is oblivious to their danger. And then Israel, blind to God's goodness, turns away from him to follow Baal. Nevertheless, God is still quick to forgive and continue his covenant[2] purposes in Israel. The unconditional, undeserved, unfailing love of God is beautifully displayed in these events.

Whole-Bible Connections

BAAL. Of 67 appearances in Bible, this is the first time Baal is mentioned. The lust of the people after this false god and their quickness to abandon Yahweh, as described in this first encounter with Baal, is an archetype for Israel's subsequent temptations to serve Baal—and of God's remarkable patience to forgive and restore Israel.

BALAAM'S GREED. Some scholars believe that Balaam was a distant relative of Israel. Numbers 22:5 notes that Balaam came from "Pethor, which is near the [Euphrates] River in the land of the people of Amaw." The Hebrew "Amaw" could be translated "his people." Thus this verse might mean that Balaam was from "the land of the sons of his [i.e., Israel's] people." Balaam could be a descendant of Abraham's kin from that region, the household of Bethuel and Laban (Gen. 24:1–61). Perhaps Balak recruited Balaam, rather than using a shaman of his own religion, because Balaam knew the same God that Israel served. Whatever Balaam's background, it is clear that he knew Yahweh but was willing to abandon faithfulness for the sake of gain. This willingness to apostatize[3] for the sake of wealth becomes known in the Bible as "the way of Balaam, the son of Beor, who loved gain from wrongdoing" (2 Pet. 2:15; compare Jude 11).

Theological Soundings

THE PROMISED KING. Balaam prophesied before Israel set foot in the land, yet he anticipated the rise of an Israelite dynasty to rule the whole land (Num. 24:17). This probably refers to the rise of King David, who completed Israel's conquest of the land. Some believe the reference is more precisely to Jesus, the Son of David. The mention of a star to mark this promised king has often been compared to the star of Bethlehem (Matt. 2:2). While the latter interpretation is attractive, the reference is most likely to the rise of the Davidic dynasty generally (compare Gen. 49:10). The Pentateuch reveals a prominent interest in the tribe of Judah and the Davidic dynasty, which, of course, is the line from which the Messiah was to appear.

Personal Implications

Use the space below to help you reflect on these final events of the exodus generation, and lessons the Spirit impresses on your heart regarding this text's (1) *Gospel Glimpses*, (2) *Whole-Bible Connections*, (3) *Theological Soundings*, and (4) the story as a whole.

1. Gospel Glimpses

2. Whole-Bible Connections

3. Theological Soundings

4. Numbers 22:1–25:18

▶ As You Finish This Unit . . .

Pray for God's grace to learn the lessons of Balaam and Baal-Peor, that you might resist the allure of idolatry and trust in his great, abiding love.

Definitions

[1] **Oracle** – From Latin "to speak." In the Bible, refers to a divine pronouncement delivered through a human agent.

[2] **Covenant** – A binding agreement between two parties, typically involving a formal statement of their relationship, a list of stipulations and obligations for both parties, a list of witnesses to the agreement, and a list of curses for unfaithfulness and blessings for faithfulness to the agreement. The OT is more properly understood as the old covenant, meaning the agreement established between God and his people prior to the coming of Jesus Christ and the establishment of the new covenant (the NT).

[3] **Apostasy** – Abandonment or renunciation of professed faith.

WEEK 9: A FAITHFUL GENERATION, AT LAST

Numbers 26:1–30:16

▲

Typically, an older generation is known for wisdom while a younger generation tends toward folly. The book of Numbers, however, confronts us with the opposite: here the older generation is stubborn and marked by folly whereas the new generation learns from its parents' failures, demonstrates remarkable faithfulness, and experiences great victories. Numbers introduces this new generation with the book's second census (26:1–65). The previous census (1:1–46) introduced the generation who wandered in the wilderness; the new census introduces us to a new generation—followed by a refreshing series of narratives and rituals marking its faithfulness.

The Big Picture

A faithful generation moves beyond the sins of its parents but honors and continues the godly heritage received through them.

> **Reflection and Discussion**

Read each of the following sections, pausing to interact with the provided questions after each reading. (See the notes in the *ESV Study Bible*, pages 307–314, for additional insights as you read; online at www.esv.org.)

1. A New Census for a New Generation (26:1–65)

The opening and closing verses framing the new census show that the exodus generation is gone: "after the plague" (v. 1; cf. 25:9); "among these there was not one of those listed [in the previous census]. . . . Not one of them was left" (vv. 64–65). There is even a new high priest (v. 1). As you reflect on the failures of the past generation, write down one or two key lessons you have learned that are applicable to your own spiritual walk.

Genesis 46:8–27 lists 12 sons of Jacob, with 70 members of their households on their way out of Canaan. Compare that list to this census of 12 tribes, with 70 clans preparing to enter the land. Also write down and calculate the change from the total count of the previous census (2:32 and 3:39) to the new generation's count (26:51, 62). What do these statistics of growth and stability reflect about God's dealings with Israel?

Three mini-stories are incorporated into the census report (vv. 9–11; v. 19; vv. 59–61). Each explains why certain family lines lack descendants in the present lineage. Write down any observations or lessons that you have drawn from these three mini-stories.

_____

_____

_____

_____

_____

_____

The first census (1:1–46) was an enlistment for movement and war. This second census includes clan-by-clan reckonings that were not part of the previous census. What is the distinctive purpose of this second census that explains its different system of counting? (See vv. 52–56.)

_____

_____

_____

_____

_____

_____

2. New Generation Role Models (27:1–11)

The rest of the book is framed by attention to Zelophehad's daughters, whose story begins here (27:1–11) and is revisited at the end of the book (36:1–13). Even though Zelophehad participated in his generation's stubbornness (27:3), his daughters strive to preserve the family name (v. 4). Women could already inherit property, but women who inherited would take that property into a different family upon marriage. In a family of all girls, such as Zelophehad's, the family line would come to an end. To avoid this result, God instructs Moses to "transfer the inheritance of their father to [or 'through']" these women (v. 7). When these women marry, their husbands and children will be counted as part of the women's paternal heritage. This would be akin to a man's taking his wife's surname and thereby preserving _her_ family from extinction. (See an example of this in Neh. 7:63.) Write down your thoughts concerning this remarkable model of heritage.

_____

_____

_____

_____

3. New Generation Leadership (27:12–23)

Moses is about to die, and so new leadership must be appointed. There are two offices of leadership in Israel at this time: the priesthood, to be continued by Eleazar; and overall rule, to be continued by Joshua. What are some of the specific duties assigned to Joshua as the new leader of the people (vv. 16–20)?

What are some of the duties Eleazar will carry as the new high priest (v. 21)?

4. Public Celebrations with the King (28:1–29:40)

Holidays are times of feasting with loved ones and friends. Israel's holidays were the same, with food offerings reminding them that God also "feasted" with them. The sacrifice instructions in these chapters focus on the "food offerings" (28:1–2) which represent the daily (28:3–8), weekly (28:9–10), monthly (28:11–15), and seasonal (28:16–29:39) communion of God dwelling with his people. The phrase "pleasing aroma" captures this delight of God. How many times does this term appear in these two chapters? _____

5. Private Celebrations with the King (30:1–16)

This next section outlines arrangements for individual offerings. When a person experienced a particular act of God's goodness, he or she might vow an offering of praise. It was important not to make such a vow in a moment of excitement, only to neglect it when the initial emotions subsided (compare Eccles. 5:4–6). In this passage, the basic law is given first (Num. 30:1–2), followed by a series of special situations (vv. 3–15). These example situations reassure those who, making a good faith vow to the Lord, are unable to follow through due to restrictions imposed by someone else. Such circumstances are explored, with examples of a wife or daughter whose promises of sacrifice are hindered by the head of the household (who ultimately owns the family livestock). The same principle would apply to sons or servants as well. Review the text according to the following outline, noting observations as you consider each category:

a. A daughter in her father's estate (vv. 3–5):

b. A woman who makes a vow while part of one household but moves into a different household before its fulfillment (vv. 6–9):

c. A wife in her husband's estate (to "afflict oneself" means to undertake a period of fasting) (vv. 10–15):

Read through the following three sections on *Gospel Glimpses, Whole-Bible Connections*, and *Theological Soundings*. Then take time to consider the *Personal Implications* these sections may have for you.

Gospel Glimpses

COVENANT-KEEPING GOD. It takes only one weak link for a chain to fail. It takes only one major business failure for a multigenerational family company to go under. It takes only one childless generation for a family name to die out. But the covenant-keeping grace of God, ensuring that his kingdom of grace will persist, is demonstrated profoundly in this passage, especially in the appearance of a new generation counted in the census reported in chapter 26. This is seen also in God's ordination of a new priest and a new ruler to replace Aaron and Moses for the shepherding of the new generation. It is seen further in the special arrangements appointed by God in order to ensure that the family name of Zelophehad does not lose its place in Israel. These pictures illustrate the faithfulness of God to uphold his covenant people through all ages, even in the wake of a generation as stubborn and faithless as that of the exodus.

Whole-Bible Connections

SONS OF KORAH. All of those who participated in the rebellion of Korah (studied in a previous section; 16:1–50) perished, including "all the people who belonged to Korah and all their goods" (16:32). But now, in 26:9–11, the census clarifies that "the fire devoured [the] 250 men" who had shared in Korah's rebellion, "but the sons of Korah did not die" (26:10–11). These children of the rebel Levite remained faithful to the Lord and to the priesthood of Aaron, in spite of their father's rebellion. It is probably descendants of this line who are the "sons of Korah" identified with several of the Psalms (see the headings of Psalms 42–49, 84–85, 87–88).

Theological Soundings

FAMILY. The goodness of creation, reported in the opening chapter of Genesis, climaxes with the creation of mankind. God created "man in his own image, . . . male and female he created them" (Gen. 1:27). Then he blessed them and commanded them to "be fruitful and multiply and fill the earth and subdue it, and have dominion over . . . the earth" (Gen. 1:28). God created the family as the cornerstone of society, and family-centered society as the structure for human stewardship of the earth and its fruitfulness. The family is not merely a practicality. God ordained the family to be the fundamental realm wherein his likeness as a God of love is to be displayed and from which his love is to be learned and further reflected between neighbors and extended social institutions. Other social experiments have been attempted throughout history, and many science fiction novels envision societies organized around other patterns besides the family. But the nature of a family is one of shared identity and love, thereby indicating God's design for love—not other principles of communion—as the foundation of communities. The genealogies and censuses of the Bible (as in Num. 26:1–65) contribute to this important doctrine of the family in God's Word.

VOWS. The laws concerning vows in Numbers 30:1–16 are often misunderstood, since the English word *vow* is typically restricted to commitments such as wedding vows or ordination vows. However, in the Bible a vow is typically the promise of a person to bring an offering of special praise or thanks to God in response to some display of his kindness. Most Israelites lived at a distance from the sanctuary[1] or for other reasons would not be able to drop everything and take a sacrifice to the altar on the day they received God's special care. Thus, in the moment God's kindness occurred or was recognized, the worshiper might engage in prayers of thanksgiving expressing their purpose (i.e., "vow") to bring an offering to God's house suitable to express the reality of that gratitude. The laws in Numbers 30:1–16 lay out some of the basic parameters for that practice and serve to remind us of the importance of remembering to show our gratitude and commitment to the Lord.

Personal Implications

Take time to reflect on the lessons of Numbers 26:1–30:16 as they relate to your own faith today. Make notes below on personal implications of (1) the *Gospel Glimpses*, (2) the *Whole-Bible Connections*, (3) the *Theological Soundings*, and (4) this passage as a whole.

1. Gospel Glimpses

2. Whole-Bible Connections

3. Theological Soundings

4. Numbers 26:1–30:16

As You Finish This Unit . . .

How far back can you trace your family heritage? How many of your forefathers walked faithfully with the Lord? What examples of godlessness in your own heritage stir you to greater faithfulness in your generation? If not in your own family, how about in your local church? Reflect upon your own heritage, and pray for God to use this study in Numbers 26:1–30:16 to make you a faithful name in your family tree.

Definitions

[1] **Sanctuary** – In the Bible, a place set aside as holy because of God's presence there. The inner sanctuary of the tabernacle (and later the temple) was called the Most Holy Place.

WEEK 10: A TASTE OF SETTLEMENT

Numbers 31:1–32:42

▲

The stubborn generation is gone, and a faithful generation has arisen. In this passage, Moses begins to prepare the new generation to enter and settle the land. He teaches them the conduct of war (Num. 31:1–54) and the rules of settlement after conquest (32:1–42). Many features in this passage are troubling to some readers. War is always a terrible matter, and aspects of its prosecution openly recorded in these paragraphs are intended to sober us. There are always two sides to every work of judgment: visiting the wicked with condemnation and visiting the righteous with their reward. The conquest of Canaan shows both sides of God's judgment. These events in Canaan serve to foreshadow what God will one day bring about in his final judgment upon the whole world. As we study this passage, God's Word sobers and comforts us in preparation for that coming consummation of his kingdom.

The Big Picture

God's judgment brings condemnation to the unrepentant and rest to those forgiven through his atonement.

> **Reflection and Discussion**

Read about Israel's war with Midian and their initial settlement arrangements in the sections indicated below, responding to the questions provided after each reading segment. (See the notes in the *ESV Study Bible*, pages 314–317, for additional insights as you read; available online at www.esv.org.)

Divine Judgment upon Midian (31:1–12)

In a previous passage, we read that the Moabites and the Midianites worked together to undermine Israel (22:7). The Moabite plot was to curse Israel, but that plot failed (22:8–24:25). The Midianite strategy was to entice Israel to intermarry with them and to worship their gods (25:1–3). That plot nearly succeeded, and the Lord judged Israel for sinning with Midian. He would have utterly destroyed Israel had not Phineas the priest interceded (25:7–13). Only after Israel's judgment was satisfied through atonement did the Lord call for the judgment of Midian. Who was the offended party in Midian's sin (31:3; compare v. 6)?

Read Paul's instruction in Romans 12:19 concerning revenge. How does the example of God's vengeance in this week's passage relate to Paul's instructions for Christians to forgo revenge?

The End of Midian (31:13–54)

Midian had deployed its women to seduce Israel (Num. 31:16; cf. 25:1). There-fore, Midian's women will share in heaven's justice. In fact, the execution for-mula in 31:17–18 will bring the full end of all Midianite households. By sparing only unmarried girls, the design is to ensure that the *name* of Midian comes to a final end (compare Pss. 83:4; 109:13). (Note: surviving women were strictly protected from sexual abuse; Deut. 21:10–14.) What should such finality teach us about the seriousness of idolatry?

Normally, warriors kept victory spoils for themselves. But the Lord gives Moses different instructions for dividing the Midianite plunder and for ritually purify-ing it. How do these patterns of distribution guard against greed and promote worship instead?

Remarkably, God's judgment brings a complete end to Midian (i.e., Transjordan: there were other Midianite nations not included in this judgment; Ex. 2:15–22; Judg. 6:1–6), while not a single person from Israel perished (Num. 31:48–54). The commanders are astounded at this result. It is not because Israel is inno-cent (25:1–18) that she survives, but because she had been atoned for (31:50; compare 25:13). How should this outcome both sober and comfort our witness to the coming final judgment?

Early Settlement Negotiations (32:1–42)

In this passage, we learn something remarkable about the new generation: they are teachable. The previous generation always stiffened their neck and resisted correction; in this new generation, the leaders of Reuben and Gad accept rebuke and change course. What, specifically, is the original proposal made by these tribal leaders (vv. 1–5)?

If Reuben and Gad settle outside of Canaan, east of the Jordan, the other 10 tribes will have to conquer Canaan themselves. How is the initial refusal of Reuben and Gad to participate in the invasion of Canaan similar to the sin of the previous generation (vv. 6–14; compare 13:32 and 32:7–9)?

In response to Moses' rebuke, the Reubenites and Gadites change their proposal. How do they modify their new proposal to remove the concerns identified by Moses (vv. 16–32; compare v. 5 and vv. 17–18)?

Under the revised plan, the Reubenites and Gadites will lead the invasion effort (v. 17). Because these two tribes of fighting men will not have families or livestock in tow, they will be able to serve as shock troops at the head of the invasion force. What does this surprising twist illustrate about negotiating with an openness to rebuke and a humble willingness to modify one's plans?

Read through the following three sections on *Gospel Glimpses, Whole-Bible Connections,* and *Theological Soundings*. Then take time to consider the *Personal Implications* these sections may have for you.

Gospel Glimpses

JUDGMENT SATISFIED. God's judgments show no partiality or respect for persons (Rom. 2:6–11). When Israel sins with Midian, the same judgment is deserved by both nations. God's justice will not make exceptions for Israel. The entire nation of Israel—beginning with its leaders—deserves to perish, and God begins a plague to bring that about (Num. 25:4–5, 9). But the people of Israel repent,[1] and one of the priests executes atonement among them (25:10–13). Thus God's judgment against Israel is fully satisfied (25:8). In the judgment thereafter executed upon Midian for their role in this evil, all of Midian perishes but not a single person further among Israel dies (31:49). Such a result illustrates the full satisfaction provided through the priestly atonement on behalf of the penitent,[2] who would otherwise deserve judgment just as the world does.

Whole-Bible Connections

MIDIAN. The man for whom the Midianite peoples were named was one of the sons of Abraham by Keturah. Like the other sons of Abraham by Keturah, Midian was given his inheritance and sent to the lands of the east so that Isaac alone of Abraham's children would continue to sojourn in Canaan (Gen. 25:1–6). Later sections of Scripture identify a number of geographically separate settlements

79

as comprising "Midianites" (e.g., Gen. 37:28; Ex. 2:16; Num. 22:7; Judg. 6:1). In several of those texts, Midianites are associated with trading caravans. Some scholars conclude that the Midianites were not confined to a certain territory but may have spread out into several different centers from which they operated trading caravans. If this is correct, it would explain why Moses' own wife came from a Midianite settlement located in Sinai (Ex. 2:16); why Moses' brother-in-law (as part of a caravanning people) would have known routes and ideal staging locations and so served as an excellent guide for Moses (Num. 10:31); and why, despite the complete annihilation of the Transjordan Midianites in Numbers 31, another Midianite population appears later in history to harass Israel in the time of Gideon (Judges 6).

TRANSJORDAN ISRAEL. The borders of the land of promise were natural borders. Its western border was the Mediterranean Sea coast. Its southern border was the Negeb Desert. Its northern border was the mountains of Lebanon. Its eastern border was the Arabah—that part of the Rift Valley in which water from Mount Hermon pooled in the Sea of Galilee and flowed through the Jordan River into the Dead Sea. (For the exact borders of the Promised Land, see Num. 34:1–15.) When the tribes of Reuben and Gad request to settle in territory on the east side of the Jordan, they are initially proposing settlement in a land naturally defined as a separate domain and outside of the Promised Land, thus implying their willingness to be considered a separate people (32:5–7). However, an arrangement is agreed upon whereby Reuben and Gad would remain united with the rest of Israel and continue to participate in the national life of Israel. But the Jordan River would continue to inject a natural boundary between the Transjordan tribes and those inside Canaan. After the conquest was finished, questions about the nation's unity across that border would emerge and require reaffirmation (Josh. 22:10–34).

 Theological Soundings

HUMILITY. The initial settlement proposal of Reuben and Gad was poorly considered and would have brought disaster upon the whole nation. Moses was angry with the leaders of those two tribes and he vigorously rebuked them. If they were to continue on this path, they would "increase still more the fierce anger of the LORD against Israel!" (32:14). When Moses brought such rebukes against the previous generation, the heads of Israel consistently dug in their heels and persisted in their pride. But the humility of the new generation of Israel's leaders is remarkable. Even though their plans have been published, the elders of Reuben and Gad have the humility to abandon their direction and to develop a new proposal based on the correction Moses gives them. The grace of humility is an important feature of the Christian faith.

> ## Personal Implications

There are sobering lessons in this week's readings. But there are also heartening encouragements here. Reflect on these passages and note below your personal applications from (1) the *Gospel Glimpses*, (2) the *Whole-Bible Connections*, (3) the *Theological Soundings*, and (4) this passage as a whole.

1. Gospel Glimpses

2. Whole-Bible Connections

3. Theological Soundings

4. Numbers 31:1–32:42

> ## As You Finish This Unit . . .

Praise God for his patience with stubborn generations like that of the exodus and his sanctifying grace in godly generations like that of the settlement. Pray for God to foster the humility in your heart that would make you among those blessed with obedience and teachable before his Word.

Definitions

[1] **Repentance** – A complete change of heart and mind regarding one's overall attitude toward God or one's individual actions. True regeneration and conversion is always accompanied by repentance.

[2] **Penitence** – The condition of being repentant and sorrowful for wrongdoing.

WEEK 11: REVIEW AND PROSPECT

Numbers 33:1–36:13

▲

The book of Numbers ends with a faithful generation poised on the border, ready to enter the Promised Land. In this final section of the book, the entire trip from Egypt to Moab is reviewed (33:1–49), and then three sets of instructions for inheriting the land are provided (33:50–35:34). Finally, the daughters of Zelophehad reappear (36:1–13). We have met these five sisters before—the entire latter half of Numbers after the second census (26:1–65) is bookended by the story of these godly women (27:1–11 and 36:1–13). By framing the new generation's story with laws about the inheritance of Zelophehad's daughters, Numbers is presenting these women as exemplars of the faithful who inherit from the Lord.

The Big Picture

The Lord will grant his people an inheritance in the land he has promised them.

> ## Reflection and Discussion

Read each of the passages indicated below, pausing to interact with the reflection prompts provided. The first selection (33:1–49) may be the most difficult to read, as it contains a travelogue with many strange place names. Pay particular attention to the short stories included at two points in the travelogue, and count how many locations are listed. (See the notes in the *ESV Study Bible*, pages 317–323, for additional insights as you read; available online at www.esv.org.)

1. Reviewing the Journey (33:1–49)

This travelogue encompasses the entire journey from Exodus 12:1 through Numbers 22:1, "stage by stage" (v. 2). Discounting the departure site of Rameses (v. 3) and the two named sites locating "the plains of Moab" at Israel's arrival (v. 49), how many locations are listed? _____ Dividing that number by the people's 40 years of wandering, how many staging encampments per year are listed, on average? _____

The travelogue is divided into two parts, each introduced with a short narrative and a date (see vv. 3–4 and vv. 38–40). What common themes link these two short stories?

----

2. Inheritance Instruction: Remove Idolatry (33:50–56)

This is the first of three sets of inheritance instructions that follow the travelogue. This instruction addresses driving out the idolatry of the land. What will happen to Israel if they adopt Canaanite worship (v. 56)?

----

3. Inheritance Instruction: Allot the Land (34:1–29)

The second instruction lays out the division of the land among the tribes. This section specifies the external borders of the land (vv. 1–12; see page 320 of the *ESV Study Bible*) and appoints what might be called a "boundary commission" to determine each tribe's inheritance within the land (vv. 16–29). Who are the "cochairmen" of this commission (v. 17)?

The members of the boundary commission include chiefs from only 10 of the tribes. Which two of the land-inheriting tribes are not represented, and why (see 32:1, 19)?

4. Inheritance Instruction: Levitical Cities (35:1–34)

The final inheritance instruction provides for the Levites. The other tribes receive land and cities in order to farm and build businesses, but the Levites are to be devoted to the nation's worship and education in God's ways. How will the location of the Levitical cities facilitate this calling?

The Levites will not own the cities where they settle. These cities will remain the possession of their host tribes, among whom the Levites will live. One key provision in this arrangement is the grant of exclusive use of the city's best pastureland for the Levites (vv. 3–5). What does this provision indicate about the attitude a city's economic leaders should have toward its economically non-productive Levites?

Of the 48 cities where Levites will settle, six are designated "cities of refuge" (v. 6). These cities will provide accessible locations for those accused of a capital crime to obtain a fair trial under Levitical protection. Compare the six kinds of manslaughter worthy of condemnation (vv. 16–21) with the three that are not to be avenged (vv. 22–24). What do these examples tell us about the importance of the condition of the perpetrator's heart in determining guilt?

Even accidental manslaughter is the perpetrator's responsibility. The avenger is allowed to execute the accidental killer if encountered outside the city of refuge. If the perpetrator takes up residence in the city of refuge, however, he is to be sheltered. When the current high priest dies, the high priest's blood is to be accepted by God as substitution for the accidental killer (v. 28). How does this provision of substitutionary satisfaction by the high priest illustrate the ultimate satisfaction provided by the Great High Priest, Christ Jesus?

5. New Generation Role Models, Part 2 (36:1–13)

The faithfulness of the settlement generation is modeled by the daughters of Zelophehad, whose story frames their generation's section in Numbers. Review the first half of their story (27:1–11; see the section on "New Generation Role

Models" in Week 9, above) and jot down a few notes to refresh your memory on their inheritance dilemma and how it was resolved in that passage.

In the previous passage about Zelophehad's daughters, concern for their father's name was addressed. But there remains a threat to the *clan's* interests. If these women marry into a different clan or tribe, the estate of Zelophehad would be transferred from the clan of Gilead to another clan. How does Moses instruct the women to avoid this outcome (vv. 5–8)?

In the final verses of the book, we are told how the daughters of Zelophehad honor their family and their clan heritage in their marriage decisions (vv. 10–12). Why do you suppose the book of Numbers concludes its lessons on faithfulness with the testimony of these five women?

Read through the following three sections on *Gospel Glimpses, Whole-Bible Connections*, and *Theological Soundings*. Then take time to consider the *Personal Implications* these sections may have for you.

Gospel Glimpses

SUBSTITUTIONARY PRIEST. Most Old Testament lessons on substitutionary atonement involve an animal as the model substitute. However, in a few key places the Old Testament points explicitly to the perfect human substitute: the Messiah (e.g., Gen. 22:1–14; Ps. 40:6–8, compare Heb. 10:5–7; Isa. 53:1–12). The instructions for the cities of refuge in Numbers 35:9–34 also contribute to that expectation. The accidental killer who takes refuge in a city of refuge is to remain there as long as the high priest lives. "But after the death of the high priest the manslayer may return to the land of his possession" (35:28). The high priest's death is to serve as full satisfaction on behalf of all who took refuge under him. The book of Hebrews might allude to this provision when it announces forgiveness for those who "who have fled for refuge" under the high priesthood of Jesus (Heb. 6:18).

Whole-Bible Connections

CITIES OF REFUGE. Ancient Israel had no police force. It was the responsibility of all of its citizens to protect the justice due to one another. Thus the nearest kin took the role of "kinsman redeemer"[1] in situations as varied as economic welfare (e.g., Lev. 25:25, 48) or the resolution of serious crimes such as murder. In any contest, the charged party could appeal to local judges for help. In cases where the death penalty might be issued, the law recognized that the accused party might need special protection in order to receive a fair trial. Cities of refuge allowed those pleading innocence to obtain such a trial under the oversight of the Levites. Once the trial was over, those granted lifelong asylum were placed under the protection of the high priest. The role of these special places of refuge continued to be important throughout biblical history.

Theological Soundings

ONE FAITH. Modern readers of the Bible often think of Old Testament Israel as a monolithic culture. This is inaccurate, however. The different tribes of Israel had economic disparities (e.g., Judg. 18:1; Isa. 28:1; Hos. 12:8), differences in spoken dialects (e.g., Judg. 12:5–6), and other tribal distinctions. The Old Testament histories are full of examples of tensions arising between the various tribes (e.g., Judg. 20:1–48; 2 Chron. 10:16). However, God held the tribes together in one faith through the dispersion of the Levites among them all. Rather than settling the Levites in settlements around Jerusalem, the Lord ordered the Levites to settle in key urban centers within each tribal territory. This was a practical and symbolic provision for the unity of the people of God in one faith (compare Eph. 4:4–6).

Personal Implications

As you reflect on the closing passages of the book of Numbers, jot down some thoughts below on how your faith is impacted by (1) the *Gospel Glimpses*, (2) the *Whole-Bible Connections*, (3) the *Theological Soundings*, and (4) this passage as a whole.

1. Gospel Glimpses

2. Whole-Bible Connections

3. Theological Soundings

4. Numbers 33:1–36:13

> **As You Finish This Unit . . .**

In the book of Numbers, the faithful and forgiving God of grace has spoken to you. Give thanks for his Word and offer your own words of repentance, commitment, and praise in prayer.

Definitions

[1] **Kinsman-redeemer** – In OT times, a relative in each extended family who had the responsibility to redeem—that is, to buy back—any relative's land in danger of being sold because of debt. In the book of Ruth, Boaz accepted this responsibility.

WEEK 12: SUMMARY AND CONCLUSIONS

▲

We have completed reading through the book of Numbers. In this final study, we will reflect on key lessons of the book as a whole. Discussion questions are provided to help you reflect on the *Gospel Glimpses*, *Whole-Bible Connections*, and *Theological Soundings* from throughout the book.

The Big Picture of the Book of Numbers

Numbers begins "in the wilderness of Sinai" (1:1) and ends "in the plains of Moab by the Jordan at Jericho" (36:13). From its first verse to its last, the book of Numbers traces a journey from Mount Sinai to Moab on the border of the Promised Land. But this book is not only about a physical journey. The physical journey recounted in its pages serves as the baseline for all generations of God's people to reflect on their own journeys of faith. In Old Testament Israel, the story of Numbers is the background for the Feast of Tabernacles (Lev. 23:43), and the people of Israel were to recall the lessons of Numbers in connection with that yearly festival.

At three pilgrimage festivals in Old Testament Israel, historical events served to instruct the present congregation in the ways of faith. The Feast of Passover at the beginning of the year recalled Israel's delivery from Egypt and taught every succeeding generation its own need for Passover atonement. The Feast of Weeks in the third month of the year coincided with Israel's arrival at Mount Sinai and renewed every generation in its need for God's law to sanctify them. Finally, the

Feast of Tabernacles in the seventh month recalled the lessons of God's faithfulness in the wilderness journey to the Promised Land. In other words, the lessons of the Pentateuch narratives—including Numbers—are not simply history; they are lessons intended for every generation to glean from for its own spiritual journey.

The book of Numbers is divided into two parts, with each part introduced by a census. The first census takes place in Numbers 1:1–46, introducing the exodus generation and its journey from Sinai into the wilderness. The center point of this story is Numbers 13–14, in which that generation arrives at the border of the Promised Land but fails to enter it. They fail because they disbelieve God. They are a stubborn generation that does not keep faith with God. Nevertheless—and this is the key lesson of the book—the Lord is "abounding in steadfast love" (14:18). The rebellious generation suffers for its own sins; nevertheless, even gross rebellion could not bring God's good purposes to an end. The Lord abides in faithfulness and continues to uphold his promises for his people, even in their rebellion. It is the faithfulness of the Lord that shines forth amid the dark backdrop of the exodus generation's stubbornness.

The second census takes place in Numbers 26:1–65. With this census, a new generation is introduced. It is this new generation that serves as the positive role model for readers of the book. This is a generation that has seen the rebellion of its parents and has suffered in the wilderness due to its parents' hard-heartedness. Nevertheless, this generation has learned through those experiences to delight in the faithfulness of God and to trust him. It is the faithful generation that we are encouraged to emulate, walking by faith in our own journey with the Lord.

Unfortunately, our wandering hearts are more prone to imitate the exodus generation than to repeat the faithfulness of the settlement generation. In one of the sequels to the book of Numbers, the book of Judges reports that another faithless generation arises after the generation of Joshua dies out (Judg. 2:7–10). In fact, all through Judges the theme of faithless generations continues with the further lesson that "everyone did what was right in his own eyes" because "there was no king in Israel" to shepherd them, as Moses and Joshua had done (Judg. 21:25; also 17:6; 18:1; 19:1).

Psalm 78:1–72 pulls together the full history of Israel's journey (Numbers) and settlement (Joshua–2 Samuel) in the land, distilling from that history a message of hope in the shepherding faithfulness of David's throne. Because the people continually "turned away and acted treacherously like their fathers [the exodus generation in Numbers]; . . . [God] chose David his servant . . . to shepherd Jacob his people. . . . With upright heart he shepherded them and guided them with his skillful hand" (Ps. 78:57, 70–72). In other words, the solution to our repeated faithlessness (like the exodus generation in the first half of Numbers) is the shepherding of Christ, the Son of David. The book of Numbers plays an important role in this Old Testament lesson of the abiding faithfulness of God and our need for a good shepherd like Moses—that is, Jesus Christ—to lead us in a faithful walk before the Lord.

Read through the following sections drawing together *Gospel Glimpses, Whole-Bible Connections, Theological Soundings,* and *Personal Implications* from throughout the book as a whole. Write your thoughts in response to the discussion points and questions provided.

Gospel Glimpses

Scan through your notes in response to the "Gospel Glimpses" explored in each of the preceding lessons of this study. Among these Old Testament shadows of the salvation accomplished by Christ, which is most meaningful to you at this point in your spiritual walk? Why?

The motivating plot behind the book of Numbers is the barrenness of the wilderness and the people's anticipation of the "land of milk and honey," where they would receive a home in the presence of the Lord. Discuss how this story of a physical journey ought to help us to view our eternal hope.

The word *gospel* means "good news." How has the book of Numbers—which is filled with the bad news of human rebellion—enriched your understanding of the good news of forgiveness through Christ?

> ## Whole-Bible Connections

More than 70 quotations of, or allusions to, the book of Numbers have been identified in the New Testament. Furthermore, many Psalms and Prophets of the Old Testament also draw upon the events and lessons from Numbers. Identify one or two ways in which this study of Numbers has helped you better to understand other parts of the Bible.

Fifteen Whole-Bible Connections have been noted in the preceding lessons. Many more than that could certainly be drawn from this book, but of those 15, which has been most interesting to you, and why?

The Bible is composed of 66 books written by many different human authors in various periods of history. Nevertheless, one overarching story ties them all together: the narrative of the kingdom of God and his anointed King advancing in the world. How has your study in the book of Numbers helped your understanding of the whole-Bible story of Christ and his kingdom?

Theological Soundings

Look over the various "Theological Soundings" throughout this study and revisit your notes on these lessons. Which among those noted doctrines have you found to be particularly important for your faith, and how so?

The book of Numbers presents a vivid doctrine of human nature (especially human stubbornness) and a similarly vivid doctrine of God's nature. In what ways has Numbers contributed significantly to your understanding of God and his character?

Personal Implications

As you reflect on the book of Numbers and the *Personal Implications* you have noted along the way, what has been the most significant lesson you have gained through this study?

In your own family line, were the generations of your parents and grandparents faithful or resistant to the Word of God? What insights have you gleaned from Numbers that will help you respond in *your* generation, either to turn from the faithlessness of your parents and grandparents or to continue in their faithfulness?

What are some ways in which you can pray for and encourage the next generation, in light of the lessons learned in the book of Numbers (see Ps. 78:1–8)?

▶ As You Finish Studying Numbers . . .

We rejoice with you as you finish studying the book of Numbers! May this study become part of your Christian walk of faith, day by day and week by week throughout all your life. Now we would greatly encourage you to study the Word of God on a week-by-week basis. To continue your study of the Bible, we would encourage you to consider other books in the *Knowing the Bible* series, and to visit www.knowingthebibleseries.org.

Lastly, take a moment to look back through this study. Review the notes that you have written, and the things that you have highlighted or underlined. Reflect again on the key themes that the Lord has been teaching you about himself and his Word. May these things become a treasure for you throughout your life—this we pray in the name of the Father and the Son and the Holy Spirit. Amen.